Kabunianism

&

Pneumasomatic Sickness

(Cordillera Indigenous People in the Philippines)

Janetius

Cover Design: Shilpa Thekkechangarampatt
Interior Design: Mini TC
Mishil & Js Publishing, Thrissur

ISBN: 9781514286036

1.Indigenous Studies 2. Traditional Healing
3. Culture-specific Psychology

First Printing, 2015

This book is dedicated to

indigenous people all over the world.

"Indigenous people are nature's own people"

Contents

Acknowledgements

Good things have small and modest beginnings, from a single cell originates the life of an immense complexity and from a simple thought process emerge major breakthroughs in human intellectual development. My interest in psychology and counseling began during my days at college and was nurtured by many people. However, the need to study indigenous peoples and their cultures and integrate such experiences in psychotherapy arose during my internship under Dr. Alexa Abrenica, whose association I cherish. I offer my sincere appreciation to her as I acknowledge the precious time she gave to sharpen my ideas and shape my thought process.

There are many people who cheerfully and selflessly gave their time and talent in bringing my research to completion. Dr. Pungayan and Rev. David Ganggangan deserve special mention among those who graciously offered valuable assistance, and clarifications and formed the inner circle of the research 'team'. I must also mention the wonderful assistance of Natocyod who cheerfully made arrangements for the field work and gave valuable contact information in Cordillera.

Being unfamiliar with the territory and language of the people of Cordillera, it was necessary that I should use the assistance of many others in data collection, communication and translation. I am greatly indebted to Samuel Maximo, Ramon Davas, Rev. Fajarado, Rev. Bernadette, Dilem, Angelina Tamakan, Rev. Armand Quindo and the youth of Pactil for their enthusiastic assistance in this regard, without which my research would have lost the sharpness and the clarity it requires.

I am grateful to the following scholars: Dr. Mini TC, Ms. Shilpa (NIT-Trichy), Prof. Padmanabhan and Prof. Ravishankar who helped to reshape my research work into a book. Finally, a word of admiration to all my students, whose love and support gave me the much needed impetus and the drive to succeed in bringing this work into a reality.

Preface

There is an increasing interest in the study of indigenous people and their cultural practices in the recent years, due to the pressing need for indigenous psychology and culture-specific psychotherapy. The ancient time-tested traditional approach to healing is often seen as holistic, in contrast to the Western medical models that focus solely on the physical aspect. It is a common belief among indigenous communities that illnesses are a sort of war waged by spirits, be it a witch, demon, sorcerer, a spirit of an ancestor or one's own spirit, possibly seeking retribution for acts of commission or omission. Because of this worldview, people expect healing to be brought about, not merely by technical, clinical procedures or chemical concoctions but, with customary rituals in tune with their belief system. Thus, their religio-cultural worldview plays a vital role in understanding existential problems and health practices.

The cultural diversities of indigenous communities and the need for culture-specific psychology are often neglected due to resistance from many Euro-American scholars and their lack of openness to ethno-cultural groups and ideologies. Although Western theories of human behavior originated to fit into a specific cultural context of its proponents, the diversity of cultures, the socio-economic setup and other belief systems around the globe forbade blind implementation of such theories in Asia, Africa and other similar cultures. Some Western psychologists argue that the study of culture and ethnicity belongs to the field of anthropology and psychology has nothing to do with the cultural differences in applying the theories of human behavior across cultures. Understanding the concepts of health, illness, psychological distress and other existential issues of countless ethno-cultural groups would enable mental health professionals to do quality therapy by identifying and solving many culture-specific mental health issues. So there is a need today to study the indigenous cultures and their worldview to deploy culture-specific psychotherapy.

In the realm of psychology, culture has been used to study human behavior at various levels of understanding by cultural and indigenous psychology, cross-cultural psychology, and multicultural psychology. Cross-cultural psychology tends to compare two or more cultures on a number of variables to discover similarities and differences in psychological functioning, while cultural and indigenous psychology is interested in understanding how human mind and culture define and constitute within socio-cultural contexts; further, they explore indigenous conceptions and ethno-theories, culture-specific worldviews, and collectivistic moral value systems in different parts of the globe. Multicultural psychology focuses on the psychological development among members of different groups (racial, cultural) and commonly used today to understand minorities and immigrants within a given society. Many cross-cultural psychologists, emphasize that at least some psycho-development processes are universal in nature otherwise cross-cultural comparisons would be impossible. Thus, cross-cultural approach ventures into critical and comparative study on how culture affects human behavior, to identify universal principles for psychology. The rise of cross-cultural psychology reflects a more general process of globalization in the social sciences that seeks to purify specific areas of research that have Western bias.

Yet another bottom-up approach in studying human phenomena and existential concerns is the indigenous psychology that utilizes knowledge, skills, beliefs and concepts that people have about themselves and apply them in understanding their behavior. This culture-specific, relativist perspective tends to clash with the absolutist/universalist perspective in most fields of psychology. The absolutist perspective that human behavior can be generalized all over the world is almost obsolete today. Cultural psychology believes that culture and human behaviors are inseparable and therefore no universal laws can fully explain human behavior; psychological theories grounded in one culture are likely to be limited in applicability in another culture is gaining popularity. I foresee that this century would be the time of culture-specific psychology which focuses on individual culture or indigenous groups and not concerned with cross-cultural comparisons.

Cordillera indigenous people, collectively known as *Kaigorotan* (Igorot peoples) in the Philippines live in the northern part of Luzon Island primarily in Benguet, Mountain Province, Ifugao, Abra, Apayo and Kalinga provinces. For the lowland Filipinos, all the indigenous communities in the Cordillera seem to be similar and thus the collective name Igorot was popularized; whereas, for the native Cordillera people, this collective identification does not give any meaning and they prefer to be identified by their own indigenous names and identities.

The whole Cordillera people in the Philippines could be divided into six major subgroups, namely Ibaloy of Southern Benguet Province, Kankana-ey of Northern Benguet and Western Mountain Province, Bontoc of Mountain Province, Ifugao of Ifugao Province, Kalinga of Kalinga Province, Itneg or Tingguian people of Abra and the Isneg living in Northern Apayo Province. These indigenous Cordillera communities have a homogeneous identity in socio-cultural traits, religious beliefs, and a household deity called *anito*. They are known for their rice farming and the magnificent rice-terraces in Ifugao and Mountain provinces. Although popular for their headhunting practices

iii

in the past, no communities adhere to this practice today. The traditional Cordillera religion has its own cosmology. The supreme God is often identified with the sun and lives in space, referred to as *Kabunian* and in other names as per the specific indigenous community.

Western influences arrived in the Cordillera through Christian missionaries in the early 20th century when churches, schools and hospitals were established in Benguet and Mt. Province. Missionary activities encouraged Christian practices, prayers and rituals. The alien practices were given undue preference over traditional cultural practices and thus indigenous cultural praxis became exceptionally dormant and behind the scene activities. This further paved the way for museumization of Cordillera traditional practices. Today only a small minority of people practice pure traditional native religion and the majority follow a conflated or mixed version of Christianity and native religion. In this book, the author uses the unprecedented term *Kabunianism* to name the unorganized religion of Cordillera people and their sickness *pneumasomatic*.

Taking into consideration the present need for culture-specific psychology and indigenous theories and therapy models, this book is intended to identify the emerging worldview of Cordillera indigenous people and their health concepts to integrate them with the mainstream psychology for new vistas and better psychotherapy.

Janetius, PhD.

Director
Centre for Counselling and Guidance
Sree Saraswathi Thyagaraja College
India

Chapter One

History of Medicine

&

Healing Practices

For the indigenous people, it does not matter whether healing is shamanic, faith based, magically attuned, religious, supernatural or scientific; with a simple reasoning of getting a cure, they seek help in their ailments from wherever it is possible.

The search for fullness is an innate quest of all human beings because no one escapes the unavoidable experience of limitation and brokenness. Human beings experience these brokenness at all existential levels, physical, psychological, social, intellectual, emotional and spiritual. It is a continuing struggle within the person when one is not able to integrate different aspects of existential angst and desperately looks for a solution. To give solace in this critical moments, various folklores and superstitions emerged in the society. In a similar fashion, the history of medicine started with a fusion of facts, folklores, and superstitions. Priests, shamans, magicians, soothsayers and witch doctors of the traditional and indigenous communities played a big role in alleviating various existential crisis of the people. Working with the same worldview and belief system, these traditional healers attempted to determine the causes of the person's physical and emotional distress. This is one of the reasons why traditional healers were successful even though there is no scientific, evidence-based, generalized diagnosis or treatment is readily available to them.

Relief of pain, anxiety, and stress, as well as spiritual and emotional healing, are common occurrences in shamanic and other traditional native healings. These healings are based on the belief that spiritual principles govern the life of people (Chrisman, 2001). Therefore, they believe that the condition of the soul must be addressed in order to have healing (Wurges, 2001). For example, three thousand years ago in India treatment for any illness included a consideration of the whole person including diet, yoga and meditation - a harmonious blending of body, mind and spirit. Krippner (1988) sees some similarities between shamans and other traditional healers and modern western psychotherapy. He points out that behavior therapy, hypnotherapy, psychodrama, Neuro-Linguistic Programming (NLP)[1] and similar therapies are closely parallel to the traditional native healing methods.

Conventional therapeutic approaches do focus to a certain extent on the belief systems of the clients and emphasize the importance of clients' specific thoughts and feelings. However, they follow a very different methodology and different approach for the most part than do spiritual traditions and indigenous healers (Sollod, 1993).On the other hand, under the pretext of being very scientific in its approach,

---

[1] NLP was originated by John Grinder and Richard Bandler. Integrating the verbal and behavioral patterns of Fritz Perls and his gestalt therapy and Virginia Satir's family therapy they proposed a model of excellence in their pioneering work 'The Structure of Magic'. Neuro-Linguistic Programming symbolizes the relationship between the brain, language and the body.

contemporary psychotherapy has evaded spiritual, religious or faith aspects and the related subjective experiences that are inscribed in the minds of many people. Freud's (1928) concept of religion as infantile neurosis played a major role in the shaping of contemporary psychology, as it is still one of the often cited reasons in the Western psychological traditions which view any mystical or spiritual experiences with suspicion.

Indigenous people have a vast system of knowledge, which evolved over the centuries through persistent practice, and learned from their ancestors as a mechanism to adapt them to be one with the nature and the environment. This has been repeated, tested and modified from generation to generation. Such an approach inevitably evolves from a specific worldview and strongly binds the indigenous people with their surrounding nature (Benor, 1999). Although indigenous people know about and do avail of scientific healing practices and processes, they are more in tune with their own unscientific traditional remedies as long as these practices serve their purpose and prove effective. As Ibrahim (1985) points out, "lack of understanding of one's own and one's clients' worldviews results in frustration and anxiety for both the helper and the client" (p. 629). Identifying the worldview and belief systems that lay beneath the health practices of the client would therefore enable therapists to be more effective in dealing with clients who come from varying religious and cultural beliefs.

Psychologists are becoming aware of the fact that people from different ethno-cultural groups do indeed have unique thinking, behavior and personality patterns, entirely different from what the generalized Euro-American psychological theories suggest (Trimble, 2000). Results from ethnic studies point out the possibility of new

3

vistas in conceptualizing and administering unique psychological services, evaluations and measurements, understanding mental health issues, diagnoses, and treatment based on specific culture and tradition.

Taking lead from Freud, contemporary psychotherapy attributes the causes and cures of psychological problems to biological malfunctioning, unconscious mechanisms or psychosomatic issues; such an outlook may be detrimental to the growth of psychotherapy as an effective therapeutic means in diverse cultural settings. Freud conceptualized human beings as determined organisms acted upon by physical and biological laws. Even humanistic approach sees human being as a subjective arbitrary creation and overlooks, to some extent, any religious or supernatural dimensions of life (Tart, 1987). While directive counseling and psychotherapy give the notion that the therapist is a qualified professional who can dictate to the client what is right and wrong, non-directive approaches believe that the client has the potency to change by counsel or through the realization of their inner self. In contrast with these Euro-American psychotherapeutic approaches, the traditional native healers cling to the belief system of the client and insist on divine intervention and other religious, supernatural and mystical aspects in any healing process, a practice that is appealing to millions even today.

Native healing traditions evolved in unique ways, at different times of history, based on unique worldviews and belief system. Since healing traditions are closely linked to worldview and belief system of the community, they are client-centered. These healing traditions have fastened their unique places among their cultures in developed as well as developing countries. They are often sought after as seen in the indigenous healers of Native America, the spiritual healers of

Tibet and the Himalayas, and the traditional healers of Africa and India.

In psychotherapy, culture is understood to pose a barrier to quality therapy (Santos, 1998). Therefore, an effective therapist should work in harmony with background influences of human nature, specifically the traditional cum culturally learned beliefs and worldview, environmental and geographic conditions of the clients. The difficulty faced by cultural and cross-cultural psychology is patched up by culture-specific approach. Cultural psychology considers culture as the birthplace for psychological processes and considers it as a mere tool in therapy. On the other hand, cross-cultural psychology views culture simply as a site of variations for human behavior. However, today psychologists and psychotherapists all over the world are becoming more and more aware of the need for cultural relativism[2] in psychotherapy and focus increasingly on cultural contextualization in understanding and answering human behavior and mental health issues (Cole, 1996). It is a desirable move to replace universal psychology with indigenous therapies.

History of Medicine and Healing Practices

From time immemorial human beings seek for fullness through healing whenever they experience brokenness. Healing in the traditional communities is bridging the brokenness of a person through physical, emotional and supernatural spheres. Throughout the centuries traditional healing systems used different and unique techniques of their own in bridging this brokenness by unique

---

[2] Cultural relativism is the principle that human behavior and activities should be explained only in terms of individual's culture. Originally an anthropological concept proposed by Franz Boas, it is slowly getting a strong base in psychology today.

healing systems and practices. The history of healing or medicine is therefore, a vast subject of interest, which could be contemplated but cannot be comprehensively summarized. Nevertheless, a growth pattern in the human being's search for healing may be identified and the various developments from primitive to the contemporary living using technology and scientific developments.

It is almost impossible to generalize and identify any systematic approach to diagnose and treat sickness because every culture has its own specific healing traditions. However, disease was thought to be due to either natural or supernatural causes by all cultural systems. The primitive healing techniques involved elaborate rituals and chanting mantras, dances and divination, and laying on of hands to transmit supernatural powers from the healer to the healee. Often, an elder of the clan or a priest who is considered to be wise in the practical and religious ways of people is selected or appointed as healer (Benor, 2001). However, the modern medical field looks at these traditional healings with suspicion and contempt and does not accept cures presumably caused by these healings. Of the many healing traditions of the world, shamanism, alchemy and yoga are noted for the wide variety of their followers; of these, shamanism has the widespread distribution throughout the world (Halifax, 1982).

Shamanic healing is one of the oldest healing systems still vibrant in many communities. Shamans were known for many pseudoscientific practices. Due to the fact that the role played by shamans and the healing in alleviating emotional problems, it has recently become a topic of interest for many psychologists and mental health professionals. Shamanism originally started in the hunter-gathering cultures of Siberia. However, it is not limited to its supposed place of origin, Siberia, where the classical form of shamanism is still found (Znamenski, 2003).

Various kinds of shamanism are seen throughout Central Asia, North America, Pacific Islands and Oceania. It has different forms in different cultures, depending upon the beliefs as to how supernatural powers influence human lives and their conceptions of how to please those powers in order to bring about the needed cure. In history they are known for their art of creating extraordinary phenomena like rainmaking, healing, crime detection, astrology, interpretation of dreams, communicating with the dead, and fortune telling (Klimesh, 2001). They use specified techniques for entering into trances, generally through ritual drumming, chanting, use of hallucinogenic plants to alter the consciousness of self as well as clients to foretell future, and give solutions to the many problems of people. For example, shamans in Tanzania are said to diagnose illnesses by using a divining bowl filled with water, and upon placing certain floating objects diagnose the sickness and prescribe cures based on the movement of the objects (Sigerist, 1951). In India, shamans claim to talk to the dead person's spirit and predict or answer questions of the clients. Although traditional cultures attribute all abnormal human behaviors to the possession of spirits that needs a cure, the shamans who are considered a kind of powerful personalities under the possession of spirits themselves are not considered insane rather they are admired as people of extraordinary feats. Shamans use altered state of consciousness induced by meditation, dreaming, hypnosis, or daydreaming which are similar to psychotherapy techniques, such as guided imagery, active imagination, dream work, and breathing exercises to help the people (Stone, 2002). Thus, shamanic traditions are considered the forerunner of many healing traditions, religiomagical healings as well as many therapeutic techniques in the psychology.

Faith and spiritual healing is a prolific traditional healing all over the world. It is based on the belief that there are benevolent and malevolent forces (spirits) and invoking the higher spiritual powers and appeasing them or subduing the lower powers that cause sickness through rituals and elaborate rites were considered necessary to have a cure. The term faith healing and supernatural or religious healings are not always clearly distinguishable from psychic healing or from shamanism.

The word 'spirituality' has a wide range of meanings and connotations. For a religious person it means involvement in religion and the related activities that lead towards an experience of God. However, from a broader psychological perspective spirituality is defined as transcendence in a person, holiness and searching, connection and longing (Benor, 1994a). The word spirituality is often interchangeably used to denote religiosity. A person who follows a religion and religious practices, rituals and customary functions is a person who is high in religiosity. Therefore, adherence to a religion is part of religiosity whereas spirituality has nothing to do with religion. It is about values a person holds and the moral ethical integrity one adheres. In this way, an atheist does not believe in religion or god also could be a spiritual person of high order. A person who is very high in religiosity need not be a person of spirituality. The role and meaning of religion is to lead a person to spirituality and religiosity is a carrier.

Coming back to faith healing, healings done via religion and through religious practices are sometimes labeled spiritual healing. Also the word faith and spiritual healing is also used to mean supernatural healing. All these approaches (faith, religious, supernatural, psychic, shamanic) share certain characteristics but also differ in major respects. Most faith healings combine various elements into a unitary form based on the assumption that illnesses are caused by internal or external supernatural forces, spirits and powers, when humans show irreverence or negligence towards them or, even by conflict among different forces within the person. Therefore, invoking the higher powers or appeasing the affected spirits through rituals and elaborate rites are considered necessary to affect a cure.

The role of a faith healer can be stated as that of diagnosing the illness through divination and applying the necessary remedy that often involves restoring the lost spirit of the person or removing the illness causing spirit by supplicating higher spirit or supernatural powers or by exorcising unwanted spirits together with application of medicinal herbs and drinks (Hewson, 1998). Unlike shamanism that relies more on altering consciousness, faith healings rely more on prayer, rituals, supernatural powers and other powers of the body like magnetic fields and aura. The success of these healing techniques are not well accepted and never appreciated by modern scientific medical schools because so little is understood by medical world about the effect of psychological attitudes upon the physiological conditions. However, there are certainly beneficial effects seen at least in some specific cases where the psychological powers released during these rituals have resulted in biological healings. Reliance on such faith healings through a healer can still be seen in tribal cultures in every continent.

Herbal healing is an inseparable part of tribal community's daily chores. In the tribal as well as primitive cultures, the mixture of herbal portions together with religious rituals, rites and magic like formulas are part of all healing practices. They believe in the natural and supernatural causes and the remedy invariably included a mixture of herbal concoctions and other religio-cultural elements. Women played a major role in the early developments of herbal healing among the tribal cultures, perhaps as necessity demanded of them in caring for the sick members of the family, in the tribes and those wounded in wars (Sigerist, 1951). Men, however wrote down the knowledge of the herbs and so herbal healings have been often identified with men.

There were important developments in herbal healing practices down through the centuries and the early civilizations of Egypt, Rome, Greece, Babylon, India, and China had their distinctive herbal healing practices that are well recorded. Krateus, a Greek herbalist is considered the first person to produce an illustrated work on medicinal plants (Blunt & Raphael, 1979). The medieval times reveal a progress in herbal and other healing techniques with the establishment of unconventional medical schools. In the early medieval period, with the decline of Roman culture, the Arabs seem to have developed some healing techniques, and were significantly influential in the later developments of medicine in other cultures especially in the Christian Europe. The Arabs are also credited with the first hospital established in Baghdad in 805 AD (Levey, 1966). In the medieval period, Christian monasticism helped to preserve and systematize the herbal healing traditions within their monastic institutions. From the twelfth to the fifteenth century, Italy became the centre of medicine with elaborate studies on human anatomy through dissection of human remains (Levey, 1966). Medical studies in Italy drew students from Islamic, Jewish and Christian world, and subsequently interest in medical science was aroused in other countries. In the modern times, herbal and other traditional healings have taken a rear stage with the arrival of science and technology that lead to the study of microorganisms that cause illnesses and the effective cures developed through modern scientific knowledge.

Delusive healing[3] is a therapy modality of some traditional healers who covertly perceive the sickness to be psychosomatic and induce cure using bizarre techniques and practices by deceiving the patients (Janetius, 2010). Although this healing modality is popularly believed by the people as magical healing for the simple reason that it is similar in a number of ways to magical or religiomagical healings. However, in a close exploration, the healers primarily recognize the client's problems as psychosomatic and then convincingly delude the clients by enacting the removal of various types of physical objects from the body to alleviate sickness to attain cure. These traditional healers clearly perceive the cliental problem as psychosomatic in nature, and the way they deal with the client is superb. They give an impression to the clients that healing is the work of god and do not assign any fee for the healing rather expect some payment in kind from the clients. These healers are very friendly and at the service of the clients to show their concern and care. By their friendly approach they feel one with the clients. They spend more time with the clients, not bound by appointment time and other professional concerns. Active listening is yet another important characteristic of these delusive healers; while listening they do not interrupt or contradict, do not impose their values, encourage clients to narrate their problems, patiently listen, clearly understand what the client considers the cause of sickness and then

---

[3] Janetius has identified some unique characteristics and commonality among a kind of magico-religious healing which is popular among rural communities and has categorized them as delusive healing, a unique term coined by him to denote this healers and healings. The research paper was prepared for the 2nd Conference on Integrating Traditional Healing Practices into Counselling Psychology, Psychotherapy and Psychiatry, University of KwaZulu Natal, South Africa.

try their healing modalities sometimes bizarre techniques to cure.

Although deluding the clients would stand equal to cheating, the main intention of delusive healers is the cure. This is where they differ from quacks. Lack of transparency in disclosing the nature of the problem to the client could be considered a negative mark if one looks from an ethical point of view. However, the intention of the healer is to do something (in whatever possible way) to the misfortune of the person who suffers from some problem.

Complementary Alternative Therapies

The evolution of cultural and cross-cultural studies in psychology and its impact on psychotherapy has started special focus on various complementary alternative therapies. The indigenous folk healing, herbal medicine, homeopathy, religio-magical healing, new age healing, acupuncture, naturopathy, massage, music, aroma therapy and the similar therapies of various cultures are gaining universal acceptance these days. Complementary alternative therapies are often referred to by various names as holistic medicine, unconventional treatments, indigenous healing, and folk medicine. The ancient time tested therapies like meditation, yoga, *tantra*, drumming, chanting, ecstatic dance, hypnosis, sensory deprivation, and chemical or herbal concoctions that induce altered consciousness and healing are often studied toward establishing a synthesis of ancient wisdom and modern science (Orr, 1994). Somewhat systematized therapies can be traced back to the early times of Babylonia, China, Egypt, Greece, India and Rome, which follow a wide variety of philosophies. These therapy modalities are based on some specific worldviews and socio-cultural religious contexts in identifying the causes and cures reflecting the geographical conditions of the people.

One of the reasons why people desire alternative therapies today is that these therapies stress the importance of personal action from the part of the person in need by knowing their body and mind. These therapies insist that healing is an integral act of body, emotions, mind, relationships, and spirit in a person. Complementary therapies as they are labeled, focus on the person rather than the presenting problems; it gives importance to the client as well as to the therapist rather than the therapeutic modality. Alternative therapies are therefore understood as holistic healing because healing involves the body, mind, spirit, emotions, and relationships in every disease and the therapist emphasize on caring as well as curing.

LeShan (1995) who pioneered many scientific researches into the study of alternative healing traditions identifies visualization as a common denominator among all the healers. Visualization, a form of self-hypnosis, also called guided imagery in modern day psychotherapy, is used to promote physical, mental and emotional health by imagining positive images and desired outcomes in specific situations. Visualization therapy is believed to encourage activity in the right hemisphere of the brain, related to creativity and emotions, possibly by creative imagery and self-suggestion that eventually can change emotions and have a physical effect on the body (Benor, 1993). This unifies the functions of the mind and body and brings about the healing process of the body on a physical level. Cooperstein (1992) who made a study to discover and describe the psychological and other related experiences associated with alternative complementary therapy points out that such healings involve the self-regulation of attention, physiology, and cognition, thus inducing altered awareness and reorganizing the healer's construction of cultural and personal realities. It results in:

(a) increased accessibility of subconscious material

(b) enhanced empathy

(c) heightened emotional response

(d) modified attitude

(e) altered meaning

(f) distortions in time sense

According to the same author, this is done through unorthodox, non-instrumental cultural methods like laying on of hands, shamanic trance, prayers, magnetic and mystical healing, mediumistic incorporation of spirits or discarnate entities for the communication of information relevant to healing, possession by spirits whether for actual surgical procedures or mock surgery, and shrine and 'power spot' healing etc.

In view of integrating conventional therapies with alternative medicine, Benor (1999) identifies five factors that facilitate such integration: 1) They are potent interventions that can enhance health and help to treat many illnesses which conventional medicine cannot treat. 2) Patients are sometimes dehumanized by conventional medical care, and, holistic therapies offer ways to humanize medical care; that is, conventional medicine focuses on the symptoms and disease management of medical or surgical problems of the client, while alternative therapies focus on the client as a person with problems. Complementary alternative therapists spend more time (30-120 minutes per session) with their clients, which fosters better interpersonal relationship between the therapist and clients. 3) These therapies empower the client to assume greater responsibility for self-care. 4) Awaken and nurtures intuition and supernatural awareness. 5) Focus and address the whole person - body, emotions, mind, relationships (with people, nature and the environment), and spirit - assuming that various elements are interrelated. By incorporating and encouraging cultural traditions and local philosophies to promote lifestyle changes (such as diet, meditation, yoga etc), they help the clients feel at ease.

According to Benor (1994) combining psychotherapy and traditional healing is more effective than either one alone. Many alternative healing approaches, like, biofeedback, altered consciousness, therapeutic touch, crystal healing, visualization etc. are often characterized as a transpersonal approach (Bugental & Pierson, 2001). A predominant element or factor identified in different proponents of transpersonal healing is their focus on inner states of consciousness and processes or the supernatural dimension of human behavior and existence (Michael, 2001). Although these healing modalities advocate optimal mental health through supernatural, cultural, psychological and phenomenological framework, they are often criticized for being not very scientific and non-empirical in their approach.

The map of the Philippines

Chapter Two

Worldview

&

Health Practices

Belief-systems and the worldview that the community holds is the innermost resources for healing. That is why traditional healers, ancient medicine men or priests such as curandero or shaman in the American Indian or Mexican traditions, angakok for Alaskan Eskimos, albularyo or mombaky for Filipinos, debteras in Ethiopia, delusive healers around the globe have helped people down through the centuries to achieve success in treating most disorders.

The word 'worldview' has received increasing attention for the past several years. The word worldview is the *verbum pro verbo* of the German word 'Weltanschauung' (welt meaning world, anschauung meaning outlook) used to refer to the 'wide worldview or perception' of a people, family, or person originates from the unique understanding and experience formed over several millennia. It is always reflected in living philosophy of people often seen in fundamental existential normative postulates, values, emotions, and ethics. Merriam-Webster's Dictionary (1995) defines worldview as a comprehensive conception or apprehension of the world especially from a specific standpoint. This could be further understood as how one views different aspects of life- physical, emotional, spiritual, moral, sociological and mental. It also implies that it is very specific to every individual; it differs from person to person, community to community, culture, ethnicity and race. A person's worldview is of utmost importance in giving meaning to daily life and existence.

Boyle & Andrews (1995) state worldview as a set of metaphorical explanations used by people to explain life events and offer solutions to life's problems and mysteries. Worldview is something that changes constantly and new worldviews emerge as the outlook of the society changes in the course of time. As Leith (2003) understands it, new worldviews emerge not by replacing old worldview but rather subsumes the preceding worldviews. Therefore, as the new worldview emerges, the old remains as the foundation or basis for the new worldview. The emerging worldview is, therefore, unique but still related to the old.

A worldview is generally made up of unconscious assumptions people make about the nature of realities around them. Therefore, traditional beliefs and practices of indigenous communities have a direct influence on the people today as they inherit them unconsciously. Apart from these, the elders in the community and the traditional customs they practice and talk about, influence the emerging worldview. Yet another influence in the present day indigenous psyche is the pressure of outside factors, such as, education and outside religions. Similarly, outside cultural forces do play a role in the emerging worldview.

Worldview is the living lens through which people perceive and understand human existence. The beliefs and worldview of the individuals, which stem from their communal worldview, both together form the foundation, out of which emerge health concepts and healing practices of people (Boyle & Andrews, 1995). Indigenous healing practices arise from the worldview that supernatural powers influence life, perceptions, values, and behaviors (Scott & Meyer, 1994). These traditional healing practices are slowly becoming popular in the contemporary society to the extent that they can satisfy people's needs to an extent than conventional bio-chemical therapies and therefore considered holistic therapies. This has given rise to a growing interest in studying the spirituality and other indigenous traditional healing modalities (Anderson & Worthen, 1997). Most of the contemporary psychotherapies and therapeutic techniques are based on Euro-American worldview that lack cultural relativism. However, the indigenous approaches consider the religio-cultural beliefs of the clients. Because of this, many psychologists and psychotherapists adhere to this approach and recommend the need for integration of religious and cultural worldviews of the clients in therapeutic processes.

The main identifying factor of any community is primarily the worldview. Each community develops its own system of understanding and accepting realities in life that are reflected in its culture. As Gordon (1978) points out, culture represents the way of life and thinking of groups in a society, and it consists of prescribed ways of behaving and doing, norms of conduct, beliefs and value systems. These customs are oftentimes protected and preserved to enable the communities to maintain their identity. The study of customary practices within the communities and different groups therefore would be a stepping-stone to identify the worldview of any group or people.

Each community is unique. This uniqueness arises from the existential experiences based on the geographical location, people and the historical experiences of the communities in which they live. This traditional wisdom or philosophy is passed on from one generation to the next, tested and changed over a period of time. These include language, religion, social institutions, fine arts and artistic expressions, ways of thinking and dealing with problems of life both and interpersonal relations (Hodge, Struckmann & Trost, 1975). In short, worldview may be a philosophy, a religion, an ideology, spirituality or just a way of viewing reality.

A worldview is rarely questioned because it is not perceived but rather preconceived, and people believe them by default as a basis for judging the world and reality and making choices in life. Therefore, it is unexamined, unquestioned and generally unconscious assumptions about the nature of reality (Leith, 2003).

According to Funk (2001) worldview is one's philosophy of life, mindset, outlook on life, formula for life, ideology, faith, or even religion. Therefore, it can be viewed from different perspective:

a) Epistemology: beliefs about the nature and sources of knowledge
b) Metaphysics: beliefs about ultimate reality or supernatural
c) Cosmology: beliefs about the origins of the universe, origin of life
d) Teleology: beliefs about the meaning and purpose of the universe, life
e) Theology: beliefs about the existence and nature of God

f) Anthropology: beliefs about the nature and purpose of humans

g) Axiology: beliefs about what is good and bad, what is right and wrong

Walsh and Middleton (1984) identify four ultimate questions which worldviews deal with. They are:

a) Who am I? - what is the nature, task and significance of human beings?

b) Where am I? - what is the origin and nature of the reality in which human beings find themselves?

c) What's wrong? - how can we account for the distortion and brokenness in this reality?

d) What's the remedy? - how can we alleviate this brokenness, if at all?

Worldview is neither a fixed reality nor completely expressed. Throughout history the worldview has constantly been challenged and updated with new evidence of personal experience and discovery. New worldviews thus emerge not by replacing old worldview rather subsumes the preceding worldviews (Leith, 2003). Education, religion and openness to other cultures are a few of the factors that facilitate the process of emerging new worldview, and it is a perennial process. It is an evolutionary process of belief systems, which reflects a deeper understanding of the nature of reality on personal and collective levels (Helfrich, 2002).

A worldview is basically how a person relates to the world and it is often manifested in general existential situations like decision-making, problem-solving process and conflict resolutions (Santos,

1998). The indigenous worldview therefore, is very basic and simple. People belong to the land and to be cut off from the land is to die (Kemf, 1993). Indigenous wisdom or philosophy is a way of life, bonded primarily in relationship with family, community, spirits, animals, plants, the land, nature and gods. It is an understanding and wisdom gained through generations of observation and teaching that uses signals from nature or culture and guides people in their existential struggles. The unwritten law of indigenous people is that the humans are nothing more than the trustees to the land and have a collective responsibility to preserve it (Cohen, 1996). Knudtson and Suzuki (1992) identified the following characteristics as distinguishing indigenous beliefs around the world and western belief-systems.

Indigenous Worldview

- Spirituality is imbedded in all elements of the cosmos
- Humans have responsibility for maintaining harmonious relationship with the natural world
- Reciprocity between human and natural worlds - resources are gifts
- Nature is honored routinely through daily spiritual practice
- Wisdom and ethics are derived from direct experience with the natural world
- Universe is made up of dynamic, ever-changing natural forces
- Universe is viewed as a holistic, integrative system with a unifying life force
- Time is circular with natural cycles that sustain all life
- Nature will always possess unfathomable mysteries

- Human thought, feelings and words are inextricably bound to all other aspects of the universe
- Human role is to participate in the orderly designs of nature
- Respect for elders is based on compassion and reconciliation of outer- and inner-directed knowledge
- Sense of empathy and kinship with other forms of life
- View proper human relationship with nature as a continuous two-way, transactional dialogue

Western Worldview

- Spirituality is centered in a single Supreme Being
- Humans exercise dominion over nature, use it for personal and economic gain
- Natural resources are available for unilateral human exploitation
- Spiritual practices are intermittent and set apart from daily life
- Human reason transcends the natural world and can produce insights independently
- Universe is made up of an array of static physical objects
- Universe is compartmentalized in dualistic forms and reduced to progressively smaller conceptual parts
- Time is a linear chronology of 'human progress'
- Nature is completely decipherable to the rational human mind
- Human thought, feeling and words are formed apart from the surrounding world
- Human role is to dissect, analyze and manipulate nature for own ends
- Respect for others is based on material achievement and chronological old age

- Sense of separateness and, superiority over other forms of life
- View relationship of humans to nature as a one-way, hierarchical imperative

One can easily identify a lot of uniting factors between Eastern and indigenous worldview as opposed to Western worldview. The Western world sees reality in two spheres: the upper part is the transcendent world that is the domain of gods and other supernatural powers and the lower is the empirical world, which is understood through science and the physical senses (Bailey, 1925). The Eastern worldview, however, does not hold this duality. In line with indigenous beliefs, it sees the cosmos as one reality where gods and spirits are part of the earth and part of daily living. Therefore, for the Eastern mind, religious practices or rituals have more practical relevance in daily life than science.

Jung says the West believes 'in doing' while the East in 'impassive being' (Jung, 1958, p. 560). Western culture tends to be more empirical when compared to the Eastern cultures. In the East, the spiritual dimensions are considered a normal part of daily existence. In the Western worldview, reality is 'objective'; there is constancy to the world and that it is measurable by science. Eastern worldview on the other hand stresses spiritual and transcendent aspect of life and realities. The Western philosophies and belief-systems have their focus on the outer world whereas in the East, where most religions originated, consciousness has been directed inwardly to understand the essential nature of self. As against the empirical approach of Western psychology, William James, Carl Jung, Assagioli and Abraham Maslow recognize a transpersonal approach as the central aspect of psychology.

Worldview and health concepts: Health and medicine are the two indispensable aspects of daily life in human history since time immemorial. Multitudes of factors interact among themselves that give rise to the characteristic concepts of different health systems. Cluster of beliefs, ideas and traditions further ornate, which ultimately shape the formation of specific worldviews and concepts regarding health (Ghosh, 1994). The Webster's Collegiate Dictionary (1969) defines health as 'the condition of being sound in body, mind, or soul; freedom from physical disease or pain' (p. 383). This definition simply reflects western philosophy, especially the Cartesian duality of body and mind. However, many ethno communities always consider another important aspect when it comes to health, namely, the cultural praxis.

Fullilove & Fullilove (1995) identify culture as a basic component of a person's worldview; it is constructed from a person's values; it also reflects a person's evolving history. In any given cultural setting, worldview creates security, and helps to attribute meaning to life and determines which experiences and events are meaningful and which are not. Therefore as Boyle and Andrews (1995) points out, all cultural beliefs, values regarding health care and a person's basic worldview go hand in hand. Leininger (1997) also defines health as a state of well-being that is culturally constituted and enables individuals and groups to function in their daily lives. Since health is closely related to culture, there is an increasing interest in the role of culture, race and ethnicity in different disciplines (Manoleas, 1996). Today professionally trained health care experts and therapists use scientific, rational, technical and evidence-based explanations, the roots of which are in biomedicine and the western, scientific worldview. The beliefs and explanations of indigenous systems, on the other hand, reflect their spiritual, mystical, or traditional worldviews (Leininger, 1991).

The meaning and understanding of health and disease are culturally determined (Scott & Meyer, 1994). Also, the definitions of normal or abnormal behavior are not absolute; rather, they are determined by the prevailing social norms (Tishelman& Sachs, 1998). Belief-systems, that is, the belief of faith and the worldview that a person and the community holds as the innermost cultural, spiritual, psychological resources for healing are important factors for the therapy process (Richards & Begin, 1997). That is why traditional healers, ancient medicine men or priests such as *curandero* or shaman in the American Indian or Mexican traditions, *angakok* for Alaskan Eskimos, and *albularyoor, mombaky* for Filipinos have helped people down through the centuries to achieve success in treating most disorders through a person's belief system.

Indigenous worldview: The world council of Indigenous Peoples defines indigenous people as:

> "... such population groups who, from ancient times, have inhabited the lands where they live, who are aware of having a character of their own, with social relations and means of expression that are linked to the country inherited from their ancestors, with a language of their own, and having certain essential and unique characteristics which confer upon them the strong conviction of belonging to a people, who have an identity in themselves and should thus be regarded by others" (Cohen, 1996).

From the above definition, the two significant characteristics of indigenous people are: a) descent from population groups before modern states or territories were created or defined, b) maintenance of cultural, social, economical, religious and political institutions separate from mainstream or dominant societies and cultures.

Throughout the world indigenous peoples have maintained their unique philosophy, worldviews and associated knowledge systems for centuries to explain realities, which are often ignored or undermined by modern civilization. The indigenous people and their vast knowledge are often unnoticed or under-appreciated. Eighty percent of the world's people continue to rely upon indigenous knowledge for their medical needs and two-thirds of the world's people could not survive without the foods provided through indigenous knowledge of plants, animals, insects, microbes and farming systems (Bengwayan, 19?). Realizing this value of indigenous wisdom or knowledge, many schools of inquiry strive to understand the core values and beliefs among different indigenous cultures. Traditional healing practices that are common among indigenous communities definitely reflect their worldview.

In some African cultures, where people believe that sickness can be caused by the negative forces of witchcraft, health can be restored by remedying this and by maintaining harmony with other people, spirits and ancestors such as recently departed family members by traditional healers (Hewson, 1998). Many Ethiopians believe that certain people with an evil eye can look at something and cause sickness (Hodes, 1997). In some Nigerian communities, illness is caused when a person does some wrong against another member of the community. Due to this belief, native healers encourage confession as remedy in which the patient, a relative, or a friend discloses to the healer any evil deeds the patient may have committed (Offiong, 1999). The Indian philosophical worldview that the universe is comprised of *panchabootham*, five manifestation of nature, water, fire, earth, wind, and ether is reflected in the traditional '*ayurveda*' healing practice, which is used all over India today. It advocates homeostasis between the elements of the universe in the body in order to obtain remedy for any sickness (Ramakrishna &Weisss, 1992). Filipinos believe that spirits can be used to inflict illness on another individual through the use of sorcery and therefore rural and less educated Filipinos still believe religio-magical causes as the etiology of illness (Edman & Kameoka, 1997).

Psychotherapy and religion: Psychotherapy is the treatment for emotional, behavioral, or mental problems which involves primarily verbal communication. Clients discuss the problems with the therapist who tries to understand the problems and help the individual to change distressing thoughts, feelings, or behaviors. Today many illnesses are labeled as psychosomatic and the causes are identified as psychological in nature. The distinguishing characteristic of a psychosomatic illness is the absence of physical reasons in diagnostic tests and the persistence of the symptom (Levin, 1998). The patient is unaware of this mechanism, and generally believes s/he has common sickness with painful symptoms. In this regard, religious practices and healings becomes the ultimate alternative for many people.

We can identify some similarities and differences in the approach of religious and spiritual teachers and psychotherapists. Religious teachers emphasize discipline, obedience, penance and purification as basic requirements for spiritual growth. Psychologists, on the other hand, consider practices as an escape from the demands of living in the world and encourage healthy personal growth by the process of individuation, becoming one's own authority, and exercising freedom of choice (Richards & Bergin, 1997). Since these different approaches may seem incompatible and even contradictory, it is sometimes suggested that spiritual disciplines are best undertaken after personal development is complete.

Wilber (1977) describes the human life cycle as consisting personal ego development that proceeds to psycho-spiritual development. Psychotherapy focuses on wholeness of the person as a goal, where as spirituality focuses on the inner purification leading to a state of perfection. Although the methodology may vary between psychotherapy and spirituality, the goal of both of them is often thought to be the relief of suffering; psychotherapy bringing about wholeness through counseling, and spirituality through a process of personal purification or union with God. Thus, psychotherapy and spirituality have some commonalities in their goal. Many of the processes that contribute to psychological health and well-being contribute to spiritual growth as well. The religio/spiritual practices are aimed at waking up the inner self and becoming aware of the inner nature of human life; while psychotherapy tends to work with the presenting problems by reducing pain and conflict and enhancing the capacity for better behavior and relationships.

Psychological and spiritual developments are inextricably intertwined, and both continue throughout life. Unresolved psychological issues can be addressed as a symptom of mal-adoption or inner conflict of spiritual nature. In practice, both psychotherapist and spiritual teachers do what they can to relieve suffering and help people grow in consciousness and as such both psychotherapy and spirituality contribute to personal growth and well-being. Therefore, individuals well trained in both can be of great success in helping a client. Fehring, Brennan and Keller (1987) who studied the relationship between spirituality and psychological mood indicate that spiritual well-being, existential well-being, and spiritual outlook show a strong inverse relationship with negative moods, suggesting that spiritual values may influence psychological well-being; for instance, a person's spiritual values determines how he psychologically balances suffering in life.

Miller (1990) states that psychologists should consider some form of spiritual dimension as a legitimate concern of psychosocial rehabilitation. Potts (1996) also points out that the willingness of therapists to address the spiritual dimensions of patients may greatly enhance therapeutic relationships and the efficacy of psychosocial interventions. Prest and Keller (1993) conclude that therapists 'attend to the spiritual belief systems of their clients if they are to better understand the people with whom they work' (p. 137). Since spiritual beliefs have the power to transform and maintain enormous changes in one's perceptions, values, and behaviour, it can be a source of strength in coping with physical, emotional, or environmental stress (Benor, 1994). A number of studies cited in professional journals of social work, nursing, psychology, psychiatry, and medicine all show a positive correlation between spirituality and mental health (Oxman, Freeman, & Manheimer, 1995; Halstead & Fernsler, 1994; Sullivan, 1993).

The variety of psychotherapeutic approaches available today have been broadly divided into four areas: psychoanalytic, behavioral-cognitive, humanistic, and transpersonal. Of these, only the transpersonal orientation explicitly addresses the spiritual issues. Therefore transpersonal psychotherapy emerges as a discipline not restricted to a medical model of remedial work alone but also growth oriented spiritual issues. It can also be seen as a bridge between the eastern and western belief system integrated in psychotherapy.

Transpersonal psychology: The word transpersonal comes from two words: trans (beyond or through) and persona (mask or façade). At first, transpersonal approach in psychology and psychotherapy was used broadly to refer any human experience related to religion, spirituality and mysticism (Daniels, 1998). However, today it covers a wider variety of phenomena, not necessarily religious or spiritual.

Transpersonal psychology is the study of phenomena like mystical states of consciousness, meditative practices, shamanic states, rituals etc in a psychological context (Silva, 2001). It is also a process of harmonious blending of religion and spiritual experiences in psychology. From the many definitions and views of transpersonal psychology, Lajoie & Shapiro (1992) identify the following five elements as the basic characteristics of transpersonal psychology. They are:

(a) an interest in states of consciousness
(b) concern with humanity's highest or ultimate potential
(c) human experience that goes beyond ego or personal self
(d) the idea of transcendence
(e) a spiritual dimension in human life

A transpersonal approach sees human beings as intuitive, mystical, psychic and spiritual (Hendricks & Weinhold, 1982). Psychology considers development and the formation of a stable, integrated, and individuated ego as the goal of human development and mental health whereas transpersonal psychology exceeds such description of psychological theories and explores stages of personality development that extend beyond the individual ego into transpersonal realms (Wilber, 2000). However, it is important to distinguish bizarre phenomenon from transpersonal experience or phenomenon. Daniels (1998) argues that any event or experience or phenomenon that has a transformational meaning or effect on a person can be considered subject matter for transpersonal psychology. Therefore a wide range of paranormal experiences are included in the subject matter of transpersonal psychology.

The study of transpersonal psychology starts with William James and his study of mystical experiences. James pointed out that mystical experiences are the basis or starting point for all the world's religions (James, 1936). On the contrary, while Freud dismissed mystical experiences as fantasies and regressions to a womb-like state, the behaviorists, to be empirical, ruled out the possibility of scientific study of any of these experiences. However, Carl Jung showed special interest in mystical and transpersonal issues. In contrast to Freud who labeled religion as infantile neurosis, Jung considered spiritual experiences as a sign of mental health and relief from neurosis (Jung, 1989). Jung also postulates that every human person is endowed with potentials for transpersonal and mystical experiences. His theory on personality which talks about collective unconscious, archetypes, such as self, shadow, hero, and the divine child that are related to dreams, rituals, and other symbols in life are clear signs of the mystical nature of human beings (Jung, 1958).

Abraham Maslow, the founder of humanistic psychology, is considered to be one of the pioneers of transpersonal psychology. The great importance Maslow gave to self-actualization, peak experiences and plateau experiences as the highest attainable motivations and goals of humans, place him as the great explorer of the transpersonal in human beings (Walsh & Vaughan, 1993). He sees transpersonal psychology as the logical leap beyond humanistic approach and nicknamed it '*Fourth-force*' in relation to psychoanalysis, behaviorism, and humanistic psychology, and considered it a stage higher than humanistic psychology (Hendricks & Weinhold, 1982). In the theories of Carl Rogers, Fritz Perls and Viktor Frankle too, transpersonal ideas are seen although not identified purely as such.

Besides psychologists, many scientists and great scholars in different fields have given great importance to transpersonal view of human behavior and existence: Aldous Huxley and Stan Grof who conducted investigations into altered consciousness using mescaline, LSD and other psychedelics; Teilhard de Chardin, who integrated biology with Christian theology to develop a model of cosmic consciousness; Sri Aurobindo, the Indian mystic who talked about the evolution of consciousness based on Indian philosophies; Roberto Assagioli, the founder of psychosynthesis, are just a few of the many we could mention.

Today, Ken Wilber, who integrates the philosophies and psychologies of East and West, ancient and modern, in developing his Spectrum Theory of Consciousness is one of the leading theorists in transpersonal approach in psychology. According to Wilber (1983):

> "The material body is exercised in labor with the physical-natural environment; the pranic (emotional) body is exercised in breath, sex, and feeling with other pranic bodies; the mind is exercised in linguistic communication with other minds; the soul, in psychic and subtle relationships; the spirit, in absolute relation to and as Godhead (or God-

communion and God-identity). That is, each level of the compound human individual is exercised in a complex system of ideally unobstructed relationships with the corresponding levels of structural organization in the world process at large" (pp. 35-36).

The focus of Wilber's transpersonal approach is to have a holistic approach to life and existence. Holism, according to him is the integration of body, mind and spirit; applied in transpersonal therapy, it considers healing from the point of view of the personal integration of three aspects of a person, physical, mental and spiritual (Daniels, 1997).

The transpersonal approach recognizes the importance of integrative aspects in which many disciplines like philosophy, psychiatry, counseling and psychotherapy, sociology, politics, education, anthropology, history, literary studies, religious studies, biology and physics merge together. It embraces an oriental worldview that incorporates elements of personal mysticism, oriental philosophy, and universal cosmology in proportions that vary with the theorist or practitioner (Bugental & Pierson, 2001). Thus transpersonal psychology is very much in tune with Eastern cultures and includes meditation, yoga, martial arts, shamanic healing, therapeutic touch, *raiki*, acupuncture, and other supernatural, mystical and psychic experiences.

Chapter Three

Cordillera Indigenous People

Cordillera indigenous communities have a homogeneous identity in socio-cultural traits, religious beliefs, and a household deity called anito. The traditional Cordillera religion has its own cosmic worldview. The supreme God is often identified with the sun and lives in space, referred to as Kabunian.

The Philippines is an archipelago of more than 7,000 islands that range from coral atolls to large main islands and all share a common culture. The pre-Hispanic belief system of Filipinos is animistic, filled with gods, spirits and creatures that safeguarded humans and nature. *Bathala* was considered the supreme God. There were spirits that were benevolent and malevolent. Priests and shamans were common in every village and had power over the supernatural and carried out rituals to cure physical and mental illness caused by the spirits (Miller, 1982). Islam and Christianity were imposed upon these age-old beliefs and only few indigenous communities, primarily scattered on the islands of Luzon, Mindoro and Mindanao, who have safeguarded themselves from the Spanish and American cultural infusion and continue to live a lifestyle based on their ancient belief system and ancestral philosophy of life.

Filipinos are known for their deep-rooted religious and spiritual beliefs (Calpotura, 2000). They strongly believe in the influence of spirits in day-to-day life. Belief in God, spirits and forces beyond self and a strong belief in extrasensory realities form part of their strong worldview and philosophy of life (Bulatao, 1992). Although Spanish and American philosophical and religious influence made a strong impact on the Filipino psyche, the present day Filipino psyche is not free from a pre-Spanish transpersonal worldview (Bulatao, 1992). Together with their Christian vision of life, Filipinos adhere to the traditional beliefs in the spirits, such as *anito, nuno, aswang, lamanglupa*, etc., even today (Calpotura, 2000).

In the Philippines, *Babaylan* and other religious and spiritual functionaries are often seen as traditional native healers (Fox, 1978). The *Babaylan,* a kind of shaman, in the pre-Hispanic Philippines, was mainly a woman, who was a central personality in the society in matters of culture, religion, medicine and any phenomenon of nature (Salazar, 1996). Healing is one of the important functions of the *Babaylans* and they were believed to be endowed with powers to predict the auspicious time of events, to effect healings of different kinds and to undertake and perform funeral rites for the dying. Today the *Babaylan* tradition is vanishing. However, there are numerous other traditional native healers who use complex patterns of diverse rites, prayers, rituals and other techniques like drums, dance and music to heal the people (Veneracion, 1991). *Albularyo, herbolario* (village healer) traditions are popular in many parts of the Philippines even today. They heal by herbal concoctions and prayer-based folkloric therapies. Of all these traditional healers in the Philippines, many psychic and faith healers are often exposed as fake and cheats (Raposas, 1999).

The infamous psychic surgeon Alex Orbito is well known all over the world. Orbito is also known for magnetic-healings in which he would offer healing touches to afflicted parts of the body, while the patients lie down on the floor. Orbito, a Filipino, claims that he can open patients' abdomens without any medical surgery and take out tumors and other affected body cells. After his psychic surgery, only a few drops of blood is seen in the unscarred abdomen. During an international healing visits to Toronto, Orbito was arrested by police and they found out that the blood and tissues said to have pulled from patients' abdomens were chicken parts[4]. There are many such psychic surgeons and healers hail from different part of the Philippines, who are blatant cheats. However, the native traditional healing among indigenous Cordillera people in the Northern Luzon Island is acclaimed and respected as providing alternative healing because their healing is based on their philosophy of life (Stuart, 2002).

The Cordillera mountain ranges in the Philippine Northern Luzon Island are the home of indigenous people collectively known as *Kaigorotan* - Igorot people (Ramos, 1995). Historians agree that the ancestors of Igorots originally were lowlanders who migrated to the mountains several centuries ago (Scott, 1975). This enabled them to protect and preserve their traditions and customs from the infusion of foreign cultures. Indigenous Cordillera communities have a

---

[4] Alex Orbito started his healing mission at the age of 14, when a paralyzed elderly lady claimed that she could walk after his treatment. He founded the Philippines Healers Circle Association in 1983 of which he is the President for Life. In 1999, he inaugurated the Pyramid of Asia Healing Center in the Philippines.

homogeneous identity in socio-cultural traits, religious beliefs, and a household deity called *anito*. They have complicated cosmology, mythology, folklore and unique system of religious beliefs and customs. Most of their beliefs and customs are reflected in their folklores and dancing styles (Mata, 1952). Besides these, their artistic skills are seen in utilitarian objects such as bowls, baskets, clothing and weapons. The rice terraces of Ifugao and Mountain Provinces indicate the creativity of these people. In the past decades they were known for their headhunting practices and inter-tribal fights over territory (Scott, 1975). However, they have evolved to be peace-loving people now.

The Cordillera people have physical features not very different from the lowland Filipinos. Normally they are dark bronze in colour. Traditionally they wear hand-woven special dress of their own, however they are much influenced by modern style clothing and only occasionally see them wearing traditional dress. They raise domesticated animals and fowl such as chicken, pigs, *carabaos* (buffalos) and dogs. Most of the communities live in villages that are arranged in clusters around individual gardens. The families live in small-dispersed hamlets consisting of one to several dozens of houses located near agriculturally developed areas. The basic style of family structure is extended family. Traditionally marriages are arranged while the prospective brides and grooms are still quite young (Scott, 1975). However, this custom is seldom practiced now a days. Majority of the people depend totally on the land for their livelihood as farmers and they consider themselves part of their ancestral land. The land, the ancestral domain, whose richness they have preserved and nurtured for centuries, had always been a target of colonizers in the past and of rich lowland business people in the present, who view the Cordillera Mountains as their resource base.

The Cordillera mountain ranges are comprised of six provinces: Abra, Apayao, Benguet, Ifugao, Kalinga, and Mountain Province. However, the cosmology, emerging worldview and the related indigenous health related practices of Ibaloy and Kankanæy, the Ifugao and the Bontoc native communities are the main focus here.

Benguet province has a total area of 2655 sq km with a population of 403,000[5]. Baguio City, the summer capital of the Philippines, is located in the south central part of the Benguet province. Benguet province is a plateau of about 1500 meters above sea level and has a rugged and sloping terrain, dotted with springs and traversed by rivers that drain into many valleys. The second highest mountain in the Philippines at 2930 meters, Mt. Pulog is situated in this province. From Manila, the places are easily accessible up to Baguio; however, the northern part of the province has poorly maintained narrow roads that make travel time-consuming and difficult. It has a pleasantly cool and wet climate from June to November and a dry season from November to May.

Ifugao province has a total area of 2517 sq km and a population of 191,078. Ifugao is the home of the famous *Banaue Rice Terraces*. The peaks rise as high as 2500 meters, with lush forests above the famous rice terraces. Numerous rivers and waterfalls drain into the lowland valleys. Lagawe, the capital of the province has a well-paved road connecting from Manila but once you move to the interior parts of the province, travel is less encouraging and difficult. A short dry season lasts from January to April; it experiences very heavy rainfall during the rainy season.

The Mountain province is a landlocked area in the central

---

[5] Population shown are from 2010 survey

Cordilleras with an area of 2097 sq km and a population of 154,187. Towering peaks and sharp ridges are the main features of the central and western landscape of the province. Three major rivers - Chico, Tanudan and Siffu - create three distinct valleys where the only level lands are found. The capital city of the province Bontoc is completely cut off without proper paved roads from both directions (via Ifugao or Benguet) from Manila until recently. Thus, this province is less developed when compared to the other two provinces. The climate is wet in the months of June to October and dry from November.

Benguet: Benguet province, the southernmost province of the Cordillera region has two major native communities: Ibalois and Kankanæy (Kankana-ey). Padang (1983) sees similar belief and cultural systems among Ibalois and Kankanæy. 'Benguets' is a collective term often used for the southern group of Kankana-ey, as well as the Ibaloy communities.

Kankanæy people believe in male and female godheads, as well as other spirits and believe in *Kabunian* as the creator and protector. They have a habit of saying, *'Itunin sang kabunayen'* (Thank you, God) at their fortune of events (Demetrio, et al, 1991). Often the names of supreme god and other lesser gods are recited and invoked in various rituals. They believe that the spirits live everywhere and react angrily whenever people trespass on their territory. There are also benevolent spirits, that are sought for protection against ills and misfortunes (Angelo & Reyes, 1987).

The Ibalois live mostly in the southernmost part of the Cordillera Mountains. The Ibalois are also known as Ipaway, which means people living in valleys. This community dominates the province of Benguet. The main occupation of the Ibaloy people is farming. The

Ibalois are one of the most advanced communities in Cordillera today because of their openness to modern technology and higher education.

Bontoc: The word Bontoc comes from two morphemes *bun* (heap) and *tuk* (top), which taken together means 'mountains' (Sianghio, 2002). The Bontocs live on the banks of Chico River known for its headhunting practices in decades past. The present day Bontocs are agricultural people and rarely engaged in headhunting practices. However, they have retained most of their other traditional cultural practices. The Bontoc belief system centers on a hierarchy of spirits and the supreme deity *Lumawig* is considered the creator, friend, and teacher of the Bontocs. Various ceremonies are performed throughout the year by traditional priests for a better harvest, good weather, and for physical and mental health and well-being. Although the Bontoc people believe in the *anito* or spirit of their ancestors and in spirits dwelling in nature, they are essentially monotheistic having as their supreme god *Lumawig* (Sianghio, 2002).

Bontocs strongly believe that the spirits of the deceased can communicate with the living or scare them and that they can be disturbed and offended if the places they reside in are not respected by acts such as cutting down a tree and the like. The priest is the mediator between the spirit world and people and offers sacrifice and prayers (Padang, 1983). The role of *'anito'* (spirits of the dead) is consultative. They must be consulted before every important events or decisions taken in order to maintain a peaceful co-existence with them. Ancestral *anitos* are invited to family feasts when a death occurs to ensure the well-being of the deceased soul.

Ifugao: Ifugao province, the home land of Ifugao people, is in the central part of the Cordillera region. It is known for its rich rice terraces, which in recent times have become one of the greatest attractions of the Philippines. According to mythology, the name Ifugao was derived from the term *Ipugo* (from the hill), which refers to the rice grain given to them by their supreme god *Maknongan* (Sianghio, 2002). There are also other explanations given to the name Ifugao.

The Ifugao religious beliefs are said to be the highly structured one among all tribal communities in the Cordillera. It is expressed in the numerous rites and prayers (*baki*) that tell of their gods and goddesses, supernatural beings, their ancestors and the forces of nature. Ifugaos believe that their success and failure depend entirely upon the will of gods. Therefore, they please the gods by sacrificing pigs, chickens, *carabaos* and wine. These gods and spirits that dwell in trees, stones, mountains and riversides are invoked in every ritual. Gods or spirits of ancestors often cause sickness and sufferings. The *mamah-o* (priestesses) is allowed to recite prayers to cure sickness, and this is the only ritual the priestesses perform. *Liddum* the chief mediator or the priest *mombaki* offers sacrifices of chickens or pigs.

The religion of Cordillera: Western influences arrived in the Cordillera through missionary activities in the early 20th century when schools and hospitals were established in Mt. Province and Benguet (Medina, 2000). As a result of this missionary activity, today, only a small minority practice pure traditional native religion and the majority follow a conflated or mixed version of Christianity or native religion (Pungayan & Picpican, 1978).

The traditional native religion maintains that the gods, deities and spirits have human emotions and can be appeased by sacrifice, praise and worship. The spirits are believed to live everywhere. They also believe in life after death and therefore grand rituals are performed to ensure a successful journey when a person dies (Angelo & Reyes, 1987). As Pungayan & Picpican (1978) point out, the traditional Cordilleran cosmic worldview based on the traditional religion has the following hierarchical structure. The supreme God is identified with the sun and lives in space, referred to as *Kabunian* or other names. Below is the realm of sons of supreme god and other minor deities and lower still are the spirits and deities of nature and the human community and the spirits that govern them. The life of the people is closely identified with nature that surrounds them and religious beliefs. Therefore no activity is performed without formal or informal rituals to God and the spirits requesting their assistance and every care is taken to safeguard nature which is the domain of spirits and deities. In their study among Ibalois and Kankanæys of Benguet province, Picpican and Guinaran (1981) point out some common causes of sickness. They are: natural causes like climatic changes, accidents; mental disorders and other congenital problems; sorcery or witchcraft; spirits, when disturbed, not appeased or when forgotten, or the spirit of a living person left somewhere. Lacanaria (1999) in her study on the Ibalois classifies the causes of illness as natural, religious or magical. Among the people of Bontoc sicknesses are attributed to the spirits of the dead family members or relatives and to the spirits of the sick person that remains in the self or strayed behind. The remedy for this is often offering of animals by priests (Botengan, 1994).

In general, sicknesses are considered as disharmony caused to any members in the hierarchy of deities and of nature. The cure lies principally in re-establishing harmony by prayers and offering and sacrifice of animals by local priests.

The researcher dancing with the youth of Pactil

Chapter Four

Kabunianism

The Cordillera religion is often cited and classified as animism or spiritism. Just like the religion spread over Indian sub-continent which is comprised of many different gods and beliefs and collectively called Hinduism, Kabunianism would be the apt word to classify the traditional religion over the Cordillera Mountains rather than describe it as primitive animism.

The religion of the indigenous Cordillera people is monotheistic today; they believe the supreme God to be one, whether they believe in Christian deity or Kabunian by Kankanæy and Ibalois or Maknongan by Ifugaos or Lumawig by Bontocs. A majority of the indigenous Cordillera people consider themselves Christians, and only a dwindling minority still practice traditional native religion (Regional Statistics: CAR, 2000). However in reality, a conflated version of Christian beliefs and native religion is popularly practiced in Cordillera today. Many ordinary people do not even know the difference between Christian God and *Kabunian*.

The emerging cosmic worldview of the indigenous Cordillera people has its foundation in their traditional and Christian theology as well as beliefs. The popular religious practice today which is the conflated version of Christianity and Cordillera religion is as follows: the realm of Supreme God (Christian version of God) covers the world of spirits, nature and the human domain. The world of spirits includes the Christian spirits like angels, devils, saints and other supernatural beings together with traditional nature spirits and ancestral spirits. They are viewed above human domain having control over the human domain. Nature is often identified with the world of spirits because nature is considered the domicile of different spirits. The human domain is in the lower hierarchy. Humans are related vertically to nature and to the spirit world and horizontally to the community in which they live.

Religion and education are the key influencing factors in the emerging worldview of the people concerning health concepts and healing practices. Besides these, opportunities to work outside or regular visits to other places outside Cordillera region and, accessibility to mass media are the other factors that shape their present day worldview. The emerging cosmic worldview brings out two important factors: i) the concept of religion and relationship with supernatural beings, and ii) the close ties with nature and community.

Cordillera Religion

Studies in philosophy of religion reveal that different religions came into existence when humans failed to find answers to many of their existential problems. This difficulty in perception and understanding led to speculation that made them aware of some power that governs the universe. This awareness is the essence of all religions. They started to explain the power in their own terms and thus religious fables, myths and stories came into existence. As Griffths Bede

(1982) points out, "myth is the expression of human mind and the source of all religion. One can see myth at work in the most advanced as in the most primitive religions" (p. 171). This is the case in traditional Cordillera religion too. In order to be freed from the power that governed their lives especially in the critical moments of life, they started to worship that power as supreme above all beings and thus hoped to get rid of harm (Ward, 1987).

The Cordillera religion is often cited and classified as animism or spiritism[6]. But, it is a misinterpretation by many Western and Filipino writers to label traditional beliefs as purely animism or spiritism. The New Dictionary of Religions (1995) defines animism as 'a loose, misleading designation of religion in any tribal culture' (p. 41). Spiritism is a religious belief where saints or spirits have an influence on the living (Pachter, Cloutier & Bernstein, 1995). However, there is a claim that the indigenous Cordillera religious beliefs have strong origins and inclination towards animism or spiritism. Just like Hinduism, which is comprised of many different gods and beliefs that have spread all over the Indian subcontinent, *Kabunianism* would be the apt word to classify the traditional religion that is spread over the Cordillera provinces rather than describe it as primitive animism. It is correct to say that *Kabunianism* as a religion began with polytheism, progressed to henotheism (the worship of one god without denying the existence of others), and ended in the belief in a single God.

The conflated version of religion today is, Christian God replaces *Kabunian* or *Maknongan* or *Lumawig* and the world of spirits are

---

[6] Animism and/or spiritism is the belief that everything has a soul including animals, plants, rocks, mountains, rivers, and stars; they are to be worshipped or feared or in some way attended to.

augmented by angels, devils and saints and their influence on the human domain remains the same. This version is prevalent among the indigenous Cordillera people so much so that in some places, many middle aged and elderly Christians who go to church religiously are seen actively partaking in *cañao* and other traditional rituals. Besides the world of spirits, another important aspect of Cordillera cosmic worldview is the concept of 'nature and human domain'. The human domain consists of community in connection with kith and kin and nature.

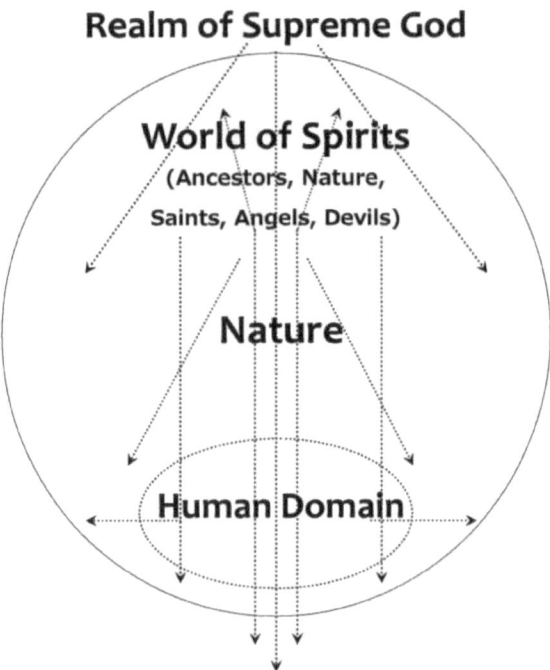

Emerging Cosmic Worldview

Kinship controls the social relationships between people in a community, governs the marital customs and regulations and determines the behavior of one individual towards another. This kinship system is like a vast network stretching horizontally in every direction to embracing everybody in a local group. It also extends vertically to include the departed because it forms a link with the 'living' dead and therefore traditionally the names of their grandparents are given to their children. All those who can trace their origin back to a common ancestor belong to the same kinship group, the members of which have a special relationship. The strong kinship relationship is evident in their communitarian celebrations (*cañao*) of butchering of animals and shared meals. Although the charm of traditional music and dance are rarely seen during the festive gatherings today, the innate spirit is still alive.

For the indigenous Cordillera people, to live one's culture means to be able to continue performing important rituals that create harmony with God, spirits, nature and ancestors and living kith and kin. It emphasizes reciprocity as far as relationship with nature is concerned. In order to express their gratitude to nature they make offerings and sacrifices, routinely, to the natural world, the spirits that govern the nature or reside in the nature in return for the benefits they derive from it. They believe that nature's bounty is a precious gift that remains intimately and inextricably embedded side by side within the human domain. Today, many traditional rituals that centered on nature are no longer practiced due to their assimilated Christian beliefs. However, nature as something sacred is emblazoned in their minds. It is from this inscribed belief that the concept that any disturbance done to nature or both living and dead relatives can cause sickness is based. According to Lacanaria, religion and education are the two major factors that influence the emerging Cordilleran worldview. As she points out,

"It is a fact that the Cordillera people are moving away from their traditional beliefs and life style. We can identify many factors. Of all the different factors that influence the present thinking of the Cordillera people, religion and education are the two main players. Mass media has changed their life style as regards dress, food etc. But, religion and education are the ones that change their thinking. The more they are educated, the more they opt for hospitals and western medicines and less traditional beliefs; the more they are close to Church, the less they go to native priests and rituals ".

Pungayan, an Ibaloy scholar and Cameyeng, a retired supervisor from Mt. Province have identified that making regular visits to other places outside Cordillera or working outside also has a very important impact in the emerging worldview of the people besides education and religion.

The emerging worldview of the people therefore is based on a cosmology that is a mixture of traditional *Kabunianism* and Christianity which accepts the Christian supreme God, Christian spirits like angels and devils together with the traditional nature and ancestral spirits. A strong tie with nature and community is still existent in this cosmic worldview. From this combination of Christian and traditional beliefs evolve their concept of sickness. The people have no specific concept of psychological sickness and all sicknesses are identified either as biogenetic or *pneumasomatic* [7] (sickness caused by spirits) or a mixture of both. Therefore, besides the traditional herbal and ritualistic healing practices, the Western medicines are also accepted as cure. The more a person is open to Western influence, less are the adherences to traditional remedies. From the above facts, it implies that culture, more specifically the client's worldview, plays a vital role in the concept of sickness,

---

[7] The author specifically uses the term pneumasomatic to refer the unique concept of sickness among cordillera people. One of the important features of the indigenous Cordilleran health concept is that any sickness not cured by doctors or medicines is inevitably interpreted as caused by spirits. Chapter Six talks in length about pneumasomatic sickness.

causes of sickness and concepts of healing which need to be considered in therapeutic interventions. As opposed to the Western concept of psychosomatic sickness, the Cordillera people have a strong concept of *pneumasomatic* sickness originating from their strong belief in spirits. The spiritual practices that includes prayer, worship and reconciliation in the form of a shared meal or *cañao* has a strong impact in any healing process among Cordillera people, which can be applied in therapy to any spiritual oriented clients.

A diviner from Ifugao (divining stick at hand)

Chapter Five

Sickness:
Causes & Cures

The definitions of health and disease, normal and abnormal are determined by the prevailing culture and social norms. DSM-IV implies that all clinicians should explain culturally the cliental problems.

Indigenous cultures around the world have developed their own explanations for illness and their own diagnostic and treatment techniques. Similarly, indigenous Cordillera communities have their own unique way of explaining illness. Although there are minor variations among different groups, they are almost the same in all the tribal communities of Cordillera.

The traditional indigenous Cordilleran health concept is derived from the mixture of religion and social traditions. Due to this fact, illnesses are not only seen in the context of individual well-being but also in the social and spiritual environment. Natural illnesses reflect the symbiosis and balance between the human being and his physical environment, while illnesses caused by supernatural forces refer to their insecurity in the community and before the supernatural. As

Pungayan, a prolific writer and linguist pointed out in an interview,

> "The worldview that accepts the influence of spirits in human life, and the need to live in harmony with nature is deeply rooted in the psyche of indigenous Cordillera people, whether Christianized, educated, or settled in urban areas. Consequently, 'interventions' focus on maintaining harmony with other people, spirits that guard nature, deceased ancestors who guide their life everyday and the god who governs life. For the Cordilleran psyche, illness is the outcome of disturbances or disharmony created by individual's relationships with their ancestors, nature in which they live, relatives and people living in the same community, healing is seen as an act of reconciliation".

More than ninety percent of the people are of the opinion that illnesses are caused by some biological causes (which can be cured by doctors and western medicine) or caused by spirits which can be cured only by prayers and customary rituals in the traditional way. As a 48 year-old respondent from Mt. Province puts it,

> "In my case, the doctors, of course, they always refer to the medicine. I'm referring to the drugs you can buy from the drugstores. For as [As for] these healers, this menkapiya (native priest) do not use them although they also refer you to the doctors, the medical doctors. Because, as I have observed, in my case, not all sickness, not all diseases maybe cured by menkapiya. Like for instance sickness like cancer or I think, I do not seen yet a person [who] has cancer going to menkapiya, as far as I can remember. Although, maybe there were persons who went to them but I don't know if they got well. There are also instances when the doctors would say, well, I think we do not see any sickness or we do not see any, as far we are concern, this patient of yours has no sickness. His blood pressure is normal, everything's normal. We do not know why he is not feeling well, but the patient complains that something's wrong with his body. So some doctors advice us that we go home and perform the rituals if you have know them or if you have what you call the "ugali". I'm referring to the customs and traditions, maybe you could perform them".

A 45 year-old Geodetic Engineer explains two kinds of sickness in this way:

"I belong to the Kalanguya tribe. There are sicknesses where in, [shall I say] the medical doctors are also helpless. Because of that, if somebody is sick and you bring him to the mambunong. It's like this: I will recite [give] a good example. You are not feeling well because as far as I could see, your late father or late grandfather or mother is complaining that in his tomb, [shall I say], the coffin had been eaten by termites or the coffin had been eaten by the ants and then it collapsed, the part of the soil covered the remains of your father. That is why he is complaining that something is wrong, so he's complaining. Maybe, you could change the coffin or you could fix it up in such a way, the coffin would be new again. Then you could bring him blankets and the usual clothing's for the dead, something like that. Because in some cases, also the living person or I shall say, the person who is sick goes to the doctor, no problem and the mambunong say, "oh, it's like this" so after that you perform the rites and you do the things and everything, the person who is sick gets well. So I would say, we go to the medical doctors they do not. . of course they give you medicines. They could give you painkillers but it can only be temporary then after that, no more".

In their study among *Ibalois* and *Kankanæys* of Benguet province, Picpican and Guinaran (1981) point out some common causes of sickness that are identical in other provinces of Cordillera. The differences are mainly linguistic and the terminology being used. For example, the supreme God *Kabunian* is called *Maknongan* in Ifugao; *mombaki* is the Ifugao name for priest and in Benguet, *mambunong* etc. Therefore, people invite priests for rituals irrespective of their community. The *Kankanæy* people invite *Ibaloy priests*; *Kalanguya* priests are invited by *Kankanæy* and *Ibaloy* people etc is a common occurrence.

Some of the common causes of sickness are: natural causes like climatic changes, accidents; mental disorders and other congenital problems (often seen in their parents or grandparents and transmitted to other members of the family); someone trying to cause illness to another person by use of sorcery or witchcraft; spirits, both nature and ancestral, when disturbed, not appeased or when forgotten, or the spirit of a living person left somewhere. Among these, the first two categories, viz., natural and hereditary are often considered biological or genetic and treated by medicines. Hereditary sickness, if not cured by the doctors, will be attributed to spirits.

Cordillera healing practices: There are three kinds of healing practices available in Cordillera today. They are:

1) herbal medicines
2) western medicines
3) traditional, customary ritual healings

Also there are two major distributions in the healing practice of the people. Those who are open to education and of Christian religions prefer to go for medical doctors (western medicines) as their first choice and if they are not cured, as a fallback alternative, turn to traditional ritual healings. For those who have no formal education, the primary option is traditional, that is, going to the diviners to identify the nature of the sickness and do the customary butchering of animals and recitation of prayers by the help of native priests. If they are not cured by these rituals, the alternative move would be to look for medical doctors and western medicines. A 43 year-old *Kankanæy* schoolteacher from Tuba, Benguet pointed out,

"Actually for us Igorots, we strongly believe the bad spirits can destroy the people and make us sick. If we are sick, preferably we go to treatment in hospital or mambunong. When we go to the hospital nearby and then if there are no findings we go to the mambunong ... Even if doctors don't believe in special Igorot rituals, they always experience like those very ill and cannot find any sickness and then go the mambunong and cured because of this. Doctors try to heal with medicine and if they know they can't find the sickness, advice [the patient] to go to the mambunong, especially if they are Igorots. They strongly believe that the bad spirits may cause the sickness. They advise the patient to go home and then do rituals".

The traditional ritual healing and related customary practices is a two-way process: a diviner identifies the cause, and according to his recommendations a priest does the butchering of animals and recitation of prayers. Besides this, there are also herbalists who are sought after, who, if the physical symptoms are well known, administer herbal medicines together with some forms of prayers as a remedy. However, only a dwindling minority opts for the herbalists today. However, a small number of Christians who believe that spirits can cause sicknesses do not use traditional ritual healing practices but rather use only western medicines.

As narrated by a 34 year-old *Ibaloy* social worker from Baguio,

"Here in the Cordillera, people believe, sometimes we get sick because of fairy or spirits. Some sickness which cannot explain, people think come from fairy and anitos. So people go to mambunong. I do not go to mambunong. I go to doctors, if I am not cured ... pray but don't go to the mambunong".

Shamanism, a common indigenous healing practice all over the world, is not an indigenous practice of Cordillera. Traditional Cordillera assumptions about medicine for illness include concepts of divination, clairvoyance, spiritism, and magical activities alongside western and herbal medicines. The people are aware of the importance of the Western doctors and Western medicines. However, they co-exist with an equally strong belief in local spirit-media and traditional ritual healing. Neither the diviners who identify and define the causes of sickness nor the priests who solemnize the butchering of animals and the ritualistic prayers can be classified as healers because their role in the cure is just mediation for divine intervention rather than healing per se. As Dr.Pungayan, an *Ibaloy* ethno scholar pointed out, "the role of the priest in the ritualistic healing is very simple, he only prays and a mediator who pleads for the people. The priests do not use any techniques like *albularyo* or any other tradition. They do not even work for money and never become rich". The people in remote barrios feel more comfortable approaching the traditional healers because they are accessible and easily approachable and the healers are paid with whatever is available. The medical doctors and the specialized system of diagnosis and treatments on the other hand, not only require arduous travel (which some are unable to undertake because of physical, geographical and/or economic reasons) but also very expensive. Farming which generates a little money and which is mostly used for meeting their everyday needs, does not allow them the luxury of setting apart a special budget for medical expenses. In other words, people cannot afford the benefits of the bio-medical system. In general, people are open to western medicines. Some people go for both traditional practices of healing as well as consulting medical doctors. They adopt a combination of the sacred and the secular. As Ganggangan, Chancellor of Baguio-Benguet Catholic Vicariate pointed out,

"The missionaries and education teach us to go for Western medicines and doctors. But the traditional wisdom focuses on prayer and rituals. Instead of saying this is correct or this is wrong, a mixture of sacred and secular is always healthy. The traditional healing practices are complementary practices and it has its own value. When both [Western medicine and ritual prayers] are done together, one complements the other".

There are three options of treatment accessible to the indigenous Cordillera people today: Herbal medicines, western medicines and ritualistic healing. The herbalist, who administers herbal concoctions together with informal prayers; the medical doctors and the administration of western bio-chemical treatment, and the diviner and priest or traditional ritual healing that involves a diviner to identify the sickness and a native priest to offer customary rituals.

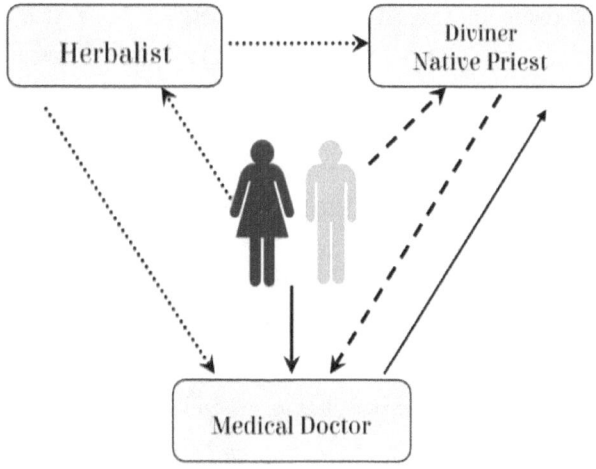

Some sick people first go to the herbalist. If they are not cured, they then go either to the medical doctors or to the diviners and native priests. For some, the first choice is diviner and native priest. If not cured, they go to a medical doctor. Some others, go to medical doctors; if they are not cured, go to the diviner and native priest. However, the western medicines and traditional healing (diviner and native priest) are the commonly preferred choices of the people. As a driver (age 36) from Benguet province pointed out during an interview:

"...when you go to the high priests (referring to native priest) and they will pray cañao [traditional rituals of prayer and animal butchering, sharing meals and having traditional dance] of course it will be cured. Sometimes, it's [illness] not cured. The doctors say that maybe it's the work of the bad spirits. Sometimes if the doctor cannot find or cure, they advise that you go home and do what you have been doing. So, for us, we go to the doctor or we go to the pagan (referring to diviner or native priest). So, you go to the doctor first. If you are cured it's alright; but if not, you can try the pagans or try the pagan first and after that go to the doctor ... the difference, if in case the spirit is within you and the spirit is the one giving your sickness, of course the mambunong (native priest) can cure you. If it is more physical, the doctors can cure you. You can't differentiate it. Sometimes it's [traditional cure] effective but sometimes it is not; sometimes both doctor and pagan [are] not effective".

There are three distinct native functionaries involved in healings:

   i) The herbalist (named differently from place to place as:
      mangilot, mengidot, menilchil)
   ii) The diviner (*mensip-ok, emanmadmad, liddium, mamah-o,
      mansublit, mantaktako, buyon, menpadpad*)
   iii) The native priest (*mambunong, mabunoy, mombaki,
      menkapiya*)

Herbalist: The indigenous Cordillera people have been recognized for their knowledge of healing herbs. Herbalists treat a wide variety of illness using different herbal concoctions and dietary prescriptions. This tradition is slowly dying due to the spread of hospitals and health care centers everywhere that compete with, if not contradict the herbalists. However, in the absence of hospitals and health care centers, especially in the remote areas, herbalists are often sought after for many illnesses. Elderly people administer herbs together with some informal prayer to *Kabunian* or to Christian gods. They do not ask for any prescribed payment. Some herbalists function as diviners and native priests too. Due to lack of interest among the younger generation, herbalist practices are now gradually dying out.

Diviner: There is no one common name for this group of people. They are called differently from place to place as: *mensip-ok, emanmadmad, liddium, mamah-o, mansublit, mantaktako, menpadpad, buyon, maonap*and and so on. Diviners are approached as the gateway to traditional ritual healing in Cordillera. Their duty is to identify the illness and the cause of the illness, using a variety of methods, from a simple one to bizarre. Some claim to have clairvoyance that enables them to tell the nature of illness. Some diviners wait for dreams to occur to identify the cause; some drop rice or paddy in a cup of water to see the movements of the bubbles, some use pendulums to divine.

A divining style of the *maonap* whom the researcher met in Ifugao is like this: he uses a small bamboo stick, roughly 10 inches long. He holds it in one hand and extends his thumb and index finger in another hand. If a spirit has affected the person who came to him, he would feel pain between his fingers. If not, he will not feel the pain. From the severity of the pain, he predicts the sickness or cause of sickness in a person. The diviners claim that they are commissioned by God or spirits or by the community and have a specific role in the welfare of the community. A 70 year-old *mensip-ok* from Mt. Province, narrated her call to become a diviner in the following way:

"In the year 1972, I had a dream in which I saw a foreign missionary complaining to me about some dirty water mixing with good spring water. When the dirty water mixed with the good water, it became a creek. The missionary gave me some oil and told me that he would make me a healer and if anyone drinks the dirty water and become sick, I can help them by the oil and cure. This dream prompted me to become a mensip-ok to help the people and I am a mensip-ok for the last 30 years".

If the diviner is a Christian, s/he prays to Jesus or to God or to any saints while divining the cause of the sickness. If they are *Kabunianists* they pray to *Kabunian* or invoke the assistance of any spirits or *anitos*. Their services are often gratis or the clients give whatever amount they can afford as a gift.

Native priest: Native Priests are often men or women who are good in praying. Pungayan & Picpican (1978) who made a study on the rituals and worship in *Kabunianism* among Benguets, identify the following factors for a person to take up priestly ministry which is the same for all the provinces of the study. They are: succession, heredity, popular choice or by constraint due to a specific need of some ailing or needy person in the community. In any such case they believe that they are commissioned by *Kabunian* to be the peoples' spiritual leaders. The native priest is a specialist in different prayers learned from their elders, parents or from another priest. There is no one name to identify these people; they are often called *mambunong, mabunoy, mombaki, menkapiya* etc, from place to place. Many scholars both foreign and local mistakenly identify the diviners and native priests as healers. But in fact, both diviners and native priests are not healers per se, for the reason that, it is not the expertise of their techniques, the magical or supernatural powers they possess that causes cure, rather, they are mere instruments of god for divine intervention. Due to this belief in prayers and rituals, many people interviewed narrated that it would be better if the medical doctors also pray for the sick person besides administering medicines.

The emerging cosmic worldview that includes the traditional belief in spirits (both nature and ancestral) together with the Christian belief in angels, saints and devils is an influential factor in their concept of illness too. Owing to this factor, a strong belief that spirits can cause illness is prevalent amongst all sectors of Cordillera people. Mainly sicknesses arise from the following sources: nature and ancestral spirits, one's own spirit, and sorcery or witchcraft. In addition, greater parts of the people believe that illness comes from two major causes: biological or by spirits. A 61 year-old narrates his concept of sickness in the following way:

> "My parents were baptized by the Belgian priests. When I am sick or my children sick, I advise them to [go to] hospital and doctors. But, sometimes if you are not cured, there is nothing to do than go to the pagan [native priest]. As a Catholic, I do not like [it]. Two years ago, my daughter was sick, she went to Baguio hospital. The doctor gave medicines and she was not cured. I do not want to try the pagan, but my neighbors forced my wife to go to pagan and my daughter was cured, when we did the ugali [native rituals]. It is not the case all [the] time. We go to doctor, only if not cured, go to the pagan priest. If sickness comes from spirits, the doctor's medicine will not work. Only ordinary sicknesses will work when doctor gives medicine. But I try always the doctor first, [if] no improvement and it is [the] spirits and I try the pagan".

If the person is not educated, every kind of sickness is understood as caused by spirits and treated in a ritualistic way. A reverse pattern is seen if the person is open to education and Christian beliefs. A 45 year-old graduate, residing in Baguio city narrates the contrasting belief between him and his uneducated father in this way:

> "... in my case, I always go to the doctors first, of course. If the sickness remains and not cured, of course, I will do the rituals, as my parents used to do when I was young. My parents being illiterate, did not go to school, both of them. During the early times, because they came from the mountains, actually they came from Tinoc [a town in Ifugao Province], and there is no hospitals. So what they do for any healing is to refer [go] to

the old folks then, there's what they call mambunong, who does the rituals and as far as I can remember, when I was a little child until his [father] death in 1990, I was then 30 plus. When I was young I could still remember he has been performing rituals, actually when somebody is sick in the family, he does some kind of prayers, I don't know if they were prayers, but he recites prayer and after that makes an observation and after sometime, maybe a couple of days I got well and then he also performs rituals in connection to the prayers that he does, the rituals, I'm referring to... we butcher chicken, one or two, for the bigger sickness, animals. The animals that are being butchered are pigs and even dogs. And eventually it becomes bigger like carabao [buffalo] and cows and so on".

The younger generations prefer scientific approach in viewing illness and other existential concerns. A 28 year-old municipal worker narrates her concept of sickness in this way:

"My parents and neighbors still believe that they get sickness from ancestors, tinmengao and other mysterious supernatural causes. I used to believe when I was small. Now that I am educated, it is hard to believe that a fairy can cause me sickness or I need tak-tako (a Cordilleran ritual to call back a person's own spirit believed to be left). As far as I know, I had never been to a native priest for any healing or ugali (customary rituals). I go to hospital when I [am] sick and I am cured. If not [cured], I consider the Doctor made mistakes in giving medicines. One time when I was sick, went to the doctor, not cured. My mother insisted me to go to the priest and do the ugali. I refused. I got well after few days. I don't say I will never go to the priest for healing. As of now, I don't".

The older folks, on the contrary, consider spirits as the prime or the only cause of sickness and seek the traditional ritualistic healings. In general, a shift from the spiritual to the scientific in their outlook is seen all over the provinces due to the emerging worldview.

Chapter Six

Pneumasomatic Sickness

The Cordillera religio-cultural worldview plays a vital role in understanding health concepts and healing practices and they have a unique concept of illness which can be classified as pneumasomatic sickness.

One of the important features of the indigenous Cordilleran health concept is that any sickness not cured by doctors or medicines is inevitably classified as caused by spirits. The researcher coins the term ***pneumasomatic***[8] to label these categories of sickness because it differs from somatization or psychologization. The concept of psychosomatic sickness does not fully explain the understanding of illness in Cordillera. In many instances, it is not 'the mind causing sickness in the body' rather any illness both physical and psychological, if not cured by doctors, is understood to be caused by spirits. Therefore, *pneumasomatic sickness* is the apt word to describe the Cordilleran understanding of sicknesses alleged to be

---

[8] Pneuma is an ancient Greek word used in a religious context for 'spirit' and soma (from Greek root) means body.

caused by spirits. Shweder & Bourne (1982) mentioned that somatization and psychologization are the two ways people express emotional distress. In somatization, distress is referred to, and expressed by the body. Psychologization is psychosocialization, that is, an unhappy situation or painful social relation that is causing pain in the mind without body symptoms. Shweder and Bourne further conclude that psychologization is a Western invention whereas somatization is closer to the norm in the rest of the world. Somatization is often referred to as psychosomatic illness.

The distinctive characteristics of psychosomatic illnesses are lack of physical reasons in diagnostic tests and the persistence of the indicators (Levin, 1998). Psychosomatic diseases are psychological diseases that manifest as somatic ones. The patient may not be aware of this mechanism, and generally believes himself/herself to be a victim of a common illness with throbbing symptoms. According to Cusani (2002), psychosomatic illnesses prompt approximately 40 to 50% of all visits to doctors of general medicine, and make up 30 to 40% of cases in emergency wards.

In the indigenous communities violation of tribal customs and taboos, such as sex, property and verbal taboos, may make a person feel guilt, which can be extremely uncomfortable and painful, and can be interpreted as a form of somatic illness (Murdock, 1980). Thus, cultural factors influence somatization and may determine the extent to which the person uses somatic complaints as a vehicle for emotional communication and social control.

In general, Cordillera people do not differentiate sicknesses as psychological or physiological. When they have problems, whether physical illness or psychological, they do not perceive it differently. Even ordinary interpersonal problems like misunderstandings among couples are often attributed to the malevolent spirits or witchcraft or disturbance from spirits. Thus, all sicknesses are seen or understood in the context of their cosmology and religious beliefs. The less physical the symptoms they see, the more they attribute the problems to be pneumasomatic.

> Ms. X is a 29-year-old unmarried girl from Mt. Province. She finished her high school in Bontoc few years ago and runs a sarisari store (petty shop) in a small village. A few years ago, a peculiar skin disease affected her. As a high school graduate and open to the western worldview, her first reaction was to look at the illness from the biological angle. After one month of treatment by the doctors she was not cured. Her mother encouraged her to seek help from the traditional ritual healing practice as a second resort. Her mother took her to a mensip-ok (diviner) to identify the cause of her illness. The mensip-ok reasoned out that the illness was caused because she was married to a tinmengao (fairy) from the nearby mountain. The remedy recommended was to go to the menkapiya (native priest) to butcher a chicken and offer prayers to appease the fairy for cure. She did the ugali (customary rituals), however, she was not cured. Meanwhile she continued applying the medicine given by the doctor. Her skin condition deteriorated. This time her mother took her to another mensip-ok and the cause was identified as her being "struck by the lightning" and the cure is to butcher a chicken and offer prayer for cure. She butchered the chicken and did the ugali once more and she felt the cure in a couple of days.

Drawing conclusions from this case, the concept that Ms. X is married by a fairy was not acceptable to her due to her educational background. Such a mystical relation with spirits is inconceivable to the younger generation. However, stuck by a lighting is easily acceptable to her and that can be cured by *ugali* (customary rituals) is deeply rooted in her psyche and therefore curing takes place. The commonly acclaimed pneumasomatic sicknesses arise from four sources:

(a) nature spirits

(b) ancestral spirits

(c) one's own spirit

(d) sorcery or witchcraft

Nature spirit: Nature is perceived as the domicile of spirits of different types, be it in a river, a tree, a field or a stone. Any disturbance carried out without acknowledging its presence can cause sickness. The following is one of the many cases, where the main cause of sickness is nature spirits.

> Mr. X is 48 years old male, Catholic, who belongs to Kankanæy community from Benguet province and presently working in Baguio City. When he was young he was asked by his parents to work in the garden near the riverbed. He, together with his friends collected big stones from the riverside for their garden. The boys started to play with the stones, throwing them here and there. That evening Mr. X had a very bad ear pain so bad that he could not sleep. He took some homemade remedies to ease the pain. His pain worsened. He was taken to the traditional ritual healing and it was identified that by breaking the stones, he disturbed the spirits. In his own words, "I might have broken the chair or furniture of the spirits while throwing stones here and there". He also confessed that he was supposed to collect stones for the garden, not to throw stones in the river or break stones and that angered the spirits that were dwelling in that area. Once he did the curative rituals by offering a chicken to appease the disturbed spirits, his ear pain disappeared.

This story may sound like a fairy tale, and in fact, it is a fairy tale to any person/outsider. However, to the Cordilleran psyche, any disturbance to the abode of spirits can cause sickness deeply rooted in their system. It can be inferred still further that nature or the river which is the backbone of their farming activities needs to be preserved and thus any disturbance is forbidden according to their traditional wisdom. Breaking this taboo can cause pneumasomatic sickness.

Ancestral spirit: The acceptance of ancestral spirits in their cosmic worldview is yet another strong factor sometimes causing pneumasomatic illness. Ancestor worship is a ritualized invocation of dead kin that has been found in various parts of the world and in various cultures. It is based on the belief that the spirits of the dead continue to dwell in the natural world and have the power to influence the fortune and fate of the living (Frazer, 1968). Picpican and Guinaran (1981) narrate,

"The ancestral spirits per se are benevolent spirits. They are expected to help the living relatives in all undertakings. They serve as guardian angels for the well being of the people. However, these ancestral spirits become malevolent: (a) when the living relatives fail to offer them sacrifices or foods, (b) when they fail to invite the unseen while eating in open spaces, (c) when they do not offer them the first juice of tapey (rice wine) before the other juice of tapey of the same jar is served and distributed to anybody... A person gets sick when he fails his obligation to his ancestors or when the Caapuan/ Caamedan needs something (e. g. blanket, clothing, turbans, or animals) from the person but he wilfully declines to give these things... A Kedeo/Kechao occurs when the ancestral spirit ask for something from the living relatives. Failure to offer these things can redound to illness or other misfortunes to the family" (pp. 97-99).

Talking to any person from Cordillera will bring out the fact that the belief in ancestral spirits is the key factor in their health concepts.

Mr. Y, a 60 year old male graduate from Ifugao province was suffering from toothache. He went to the dentist, identified his molar-teeth as the trouble shooter. The dentist removed four molar-teeth and there was no improvement in his toothache. One of the members of the family saw their deceased mother in dream, asking for cleaning of the tomb and new clothing. When they opened the tomb and checked the bones, the skull and the teeth were filled with worms. Once the bones were cleaned, a pig was butchered and customary rituals performed, Mr. Y's pain vanished.

One's own spirit: The Cordillera people have an exceptional belief that a person's spirit can be left out somewhere or it departs from the person in case of an accident or for other reasons. It can make the person sick. Often sleeping problems, lack of appetite and dullness are the major symptoms of one's spirit left out elsewhere. This may be classified as pure psychological indicators from a Western therapeutic point of view. For the people of Cordillera it is not so. It is embedded in the psyche of babies as well as grown up people; a traditional *taktako* ceremony is the undisputable cure.

This is a story of Mrs. Z, a 48-year old nurse from Benguet. She fell down and had a fracture in her right leg. The parents and relatives took her to the hospital and her leg was placed in a cast. The doctors advised her to take rest and the cast would be removed after few weeks. Nevertheless, she was not able to sleep and suffered from insomnia. She consulted the doctors and they were not able to remedy her sleeplessness. The relatives went to the diviner to identify the cause of her sickness. It was a very easy task for the diviner to identify this uncomplicated illness. As directed, the native priest did the taktako ceremony to call back the spirit and Mrs. Z was able to recover her normal sleeping patterns.

A similar story from Baguio city:

Ms. A (47) is a nurse who worked abroad (Hong Kong) for six years, married and lives with her husband and an adolescent male child. When she returned from abroad, she had some illness and underwent an operation. When she left the hospital, she was unable to sleep for many days. She was unable to identify any cause for her lack of sleep. Being a staff-nurse herself, she tried all the western medicines possible, however, her insomnia remained. The only alternative she could think of, like any other indigenous Cordillera person is to go to the diviner, identify the cause and do the ugali (customary rituals). Some of her family members meanwhile consulted the mensip-ok (diviner) and identified the cause that her spirit stayed behind, may be in the hospital. Her sleep problem was severe, and was aggravated by the conflict between her inherited belief and the adopted Christian religion and also her education and openness to western culture. Finally, a catholic priest, with whom she confessed her dilemma regarding the problem, encouraged her to do the ugali in her house rather than doing it publicly. She was cured of her insomnia when she did the customary rituals.

Sorcery and witchcraft: Compared to other pneumasomatic sicknesses, witchcraft and sorcery as cause of illness, are less in number. In majority of the cases, interpersonal problems in the family or personal problems in relationships are understood as caused by witchcraft as if someone trying to spoil the harmony of the family. The affected party becomes ill and the traditional ritual healing inevitably becomes the cure. The following is a case of witchcraft causing pneumasomatic sickness.

Mrs. W, is a 28-year old high school graduate and homemaker from La Trinidad, Benguet Province. She was married to a man for two years and had no children. Before marriage, the man was living with a lady for a few months. Recently the wife started to have problems in the relationship with her spouse and started to have dreams about the old girlfriend of her husband. Her inability to have children is attributed to witchcraft done by her husband's ex-girlfriend and the dreams tormented her. The housewife had no peace of mind and spent sleepless nights. After consulting a diviner, it was suggested that she sees a native priest and perform some rituals to safeguard her family and to get rid of her mental torture. A native priest was invited, some animals were butchered; now she can sleep well, and her fear of her husband's ex-girlfriend completely disappeared.

Lacanaria (2000) who made a study on the Ibalois of Kabayan in Benguet Province classifies people into four categories in relation to health practices.

(1) people who believe and practice

(2) people who believe but do not practice

(3) people who do not believe yet practice

(4) people who do not believe and do not practice

This classification is applicable to all the communities in Cordillera. More than eighty per cent (81.8%) of the people do believe in pneumasomatic sickness and traditional rituals as a cure. Eight per cent (8.02%) of the people do not believe in this cause and cure; a little less than two per cent (1.87%) of the population practice but do not believe and more than eight per cent (8.28%) do not practice but do believe in pneumasomatic sickness.

Religion and Cordillera Healing

Human beings have an innate urge toward personal growth, to evolve through deeper self-knowledge and feel that they are valuable elements within the grand scheme of things. Psychotherapy facilitates this issue of personal growth and integrity using specific techniques designed to encourage the communication of conflicts and providing insights into problems, with a view to the resolution of such problems by means of personal growth and behavior modification.

Religion and supernatural experiences are part of human dynamics throughout the world. Religious beliefs play a vital role in the physical as well as mental well-being of a person. Bringing spirituality or any other spiritual aspect into a therapeutic context is an ideal approach if the client believes in spiritual aspects as the driving force in life. As Frankl (1967) points out, spiritual beliefs are driven by a humanistic innate need for seeking meaning and purpose. Therefore, spiritual beliefs have the power to transform and maintain enormous changes in one's perceptions, values, and behaviors.

Over the last few years a growing number of therapists and theorists have viewed the traditional psychotherapy or the medical-model based definition of mental and emotional disorders as being too narrow and inaccurate. Recently newer models have evolved anchored on the "narratives" or "stories" that individuals relate which describes their difficulties in terms of the context and belief systems in which they occur. This paradigm shift from the therapist to the client; acknowledging that the client knows more about their own difficulty than does the therapist or counselor. Consequently, the client is considered the ultimate teller of their own story and the chief guide in the process of resolving their pain with the assistance of a therapist. Due to this, the acceptance and introduction of traditional healing practices side by side with mainstream psychotherapy is a common trend today (Levin et al., 1997). The ignored human, spiritual and religious experiences of various indigenous traditional cultures are addressed as part of the therapeutic process by transpersonal approaches (Kasprow & Scotton, 1999). Goldberg (1994) points out that anyone who is religious or spiritually inclined would find related questions relevant in therapy. The outcome of counseling and psychotherapy can be substantially enriched by the inclusion of spiritual healing (Benor, 1994a). Bergin and Payne (1991) assert that 'though working with a client's spiritual values may promote growth and change in a positive direction, the therapist should remain 'within' the client's own value system' (p. 204).

The spiritual and religious experiences of humanity, often overlooked by conventional therapeutic approaches are addressed by transpersonal approaches (Kasprow & Scotton, 1999). Transpersonal psychologists seek not only to understand the nature of transpersonal experiences but also to ease human suffering. Thus they are contributing to psychotherapy. Transpersonal psychotherapy is strongly eclectic, drawing techniques and understandings from a wide variety of psychological and spiritual sources, dealing with wide range of psychological problems, and uses a vast range of techniques, including behavior modification, cognitive restructuring, gestalt practices, psychodynamic inquiry, dream-work, art and music therapy, prayer and rituals (Richards & Bergin, 1997). Owing to this fact, Duckro et al., (1992) point out that the outcome of counseling and psychotherapy can be substantially enriched by the inclusion of spirituality. Goldberg (1994) also points out that anyone who is religious or spiritually inclined would find related questions relevant in therapy. Benson (1996) understands faith in God has a health-promoting effect.

From the traditional ritual healing practices of Indigenous Cordillera people and their worldview, the research findings bring out the strong spiritual inclination of the people and their health concepts. Healing for them is primarily divine intervention and therefore if bio-chemical medicines fail or in the absence of bio-chemical medicines, prayers and customary rituals give solace. As pointed out by many key and secondary informants in the interviews, even medical doctors in the Cordillera Region propose prayer and customary ritualistic practices if they fail to see any progress in their client by their treatments. In the words of a 62 year-old key informant from Ifugao:

> "... Doctors believe in healing with medicine. However, if they don't cure the patient after medicine, if they know they can't find the sickness in their patients, they would advise the patients to go to the native priests.

Especially, if they are from Ifugao, they strongly believe the sickness may be caused by the bad spirits or by spirits of the ancestors. They advise the patient to go home and meet the mombaki (native priest). They go and do prayer rituals and [get] cured".

Three main forms of religious practices are used as therapeutic interventions among indigenous Cordillera people.

(1) prayer
(2) worship rituals
(3) reconciliation

Prayer: Webster's New World Encyclopedia (1992) defines prayer as 'an address to divine powers, ranging from magical formula to attain a desired end, to selfless communication in meditation' (p. 903). In therapeutic setting, although there are no conclusive findings about the role of anonymous prayers in causing positive effects on a sick person, there is no doubt that people who pray or meditate do believe that they feel at ease physically and psychologically (Richards & Bergin, 1997). Benson (1996) suggests that it may be due to a placebo effect or power of body-mind connection or transcendent healing influence. Basing on a survey taken among American psychologists, Richards & Bergin (1997) discourage praying during the therapy session, pointing to the fact that it may create confusion in the minds of the clients regarding the role of the therapist as a professional therapist or religious healer. This view is a clear reflection of the Western mindset. On the other hand, for the Indigenous Cordillera people, the role of the therapist or healer in the process of healing is more of a person who prays rather than healer per se. Due to the strong belief in the *pneumasomatic* sicknesses, healing is viewed as a divine intervention by the prayers of the native priest. This spiritual remedy does work for them, if the client fails to find a cure through bio-chemical treatments.

Worship rituals: Another spiritual or religious aspect we can identify in the Cordillera traditional ritual healing practice is the importance given to worship and rituals. Webster's Encyclopedic Unabridged Dictionary (1996) defines worship as 'the formal or ceremonious rendering of honor and homage to God' (p. 2191). The Everyman Dictionary of Religion and Philosophy (1990) defines ritual 'as a patterned form of behavior, generally communal and consisting of prescribed actions and words' (p. 540). Benson (1996) points out that the rituals in human history are full of therapeutic elements. The common religious rituals used in different cultures all over the world include laying of hands, anointing, blessing, music and dancing. (Benor, 1994a). This can be seen in many organized religions as well as *religious cults,* where, heightened suggestibility often causes cure. In Cordillera Region, however, worship and rituals are part of traditional healing. Appeasing the spirits in order to be cured is a fundamental concept. The sole way of pleasing the spirits is through prayers and ritual butchering and offering of animals. Many informants narrated that while undergoing bio-chemical medicines, they also do customary rituals at home as a cure. Many educated Cordilleran consider rituals and worship as having complementary therapeutic value if done together with bio-chemical treatment.

Reconciliation: Webster's Encyclopedic Unabridged Dictionary (1996) explains reconciliation or to reconcile as 'to win over to friendliness... to bring into agreement or harmony' (p. 1612). In the religious context, it is an act of reestablishing relationship with God and people. Reconciliation follows forgiveness and repentance and, forgiveness is one of the frequently used spiritual interventions by psychotherapists (Freedman & Enright, 1996). In the Cordilleran context of sickness, when understood as *pneumasomatic*, the prayers and other rituals are focused on asking forgiveness from spirits and re-establishing harmony. *Cañao* or similar common unique ritual celebration which can be observed all over Cordillera, in which, prayers are recited, animals butchered, a meal and rice wine shared and the dancing with gongs and drums that follow is an act of forgiveness and so have the therapeutic reconciliation. Although people may not be consciously aware of the therapeutic nature of the reconciliation, this is what it signifies. As Pungayan in one of the interviews pointed out, 'in Cordillera, the cause of sickness is disharmony with any aspect of your personal, social or nature and the cure is reconciliation, often done through *Cañao* and similar rituals'.

Researcher with the Ibaloy Scholar Dr Pungayan

Chapter Seven

Shamanism in Cordillera

The distinguishing characteristic of shamans are their ecstatic trance state, in which they believe to leave the body and ascend to the sky or descend into the earth often mooted by the influence of drugs, drumming and rhythmic dancing.

When someone talks about Cordillera indigenous people in the Philippines, the first thought that comes to the mind is *mombaki* (Ifugao native priest). *Mombaki* is a term for native priests in Ifugao. In Benguet the priest is known as *mambunong* and in Mt. Province *menkapiya* etc. Always these priests are identified with healing sickness of every nature. Many western and local scholars think that these native priests are Shamans. As often misunderstood or wrongly interpreted by many scholars and researchers, shamanism is not practiced among Cordillera indigenous people and there are no indigenous shamanic healers.

Shamans are skilled healers by use of herbal concoctions and magical techniques through *shamanic journey* or *shamanic flight*. In such journeys, shamans enter a special state of consciousness and encounter spirits and return with knowledge about the particular cause of a person's illness or healing for a client or the community (Stone, 2002). One of the distinguishing characteristics of shamanism is its focus on the ecstatic trance state, in which the soul of the shaman is believed to leave the body and ascend to the sky (heavens) or descend into the earth (underworld), mooted by drumming and rhythmic dancing. This practice of shamanism is not at all seen in the Cordillera. Although a lowland Filipino shamanic tradition *Albularyo* is practiced in some parts of Cordillera, Pungayan, a prolific Ibaloy writer and linguist does not accept *Albularyo* tradition as a Cordillera indigenous practice.

In Cordillera, unlike *shamanic* healing where the priest is an active person who enters into trance and altered consciousness, the role of the priest in traditional healing process is very simple. He leads the ritual butchering of animals and offer specific prayers to specific deities or *anito* and *Kabunian*. Unlike Shamans of other cultures, the native priests in Cordillera use no specific healing techniques rather simply they leads the rituals, ceremony and prayers.

The following detailed ethnographic report of a *cañao* shows the simple role of the priest in a traditional healing ceremony.

A widow, who moved into a new house, got sick every now and then. It was identified by a diviner that the bones of her deceased husband which was left in the previous house should be moved to the new place in order to cure her illness. When the bones were moved to the new place this cañao took place.

> The cañao took place in a thickly wooded farmhouse in Bangua, Benguet Province. It started around 11:00 pm on a Monday, in the month of May. A few kerosene lamps illuminated the place. The wife of the deceased person brought her husband's old

clothes to the front side of the house where a mambunong (native priest) and a few relatives were squatting. The relatives, visitors and others were sitting at different parts of the front yard, many of them were professing Catholics, whom the researcher met during the Sunday morning Catholic Liturgy.

The mambunong (native priest) was a short, thin person. The grayish thinning hair and the wrinkled skin of his face, hands and feet indicated that he must be in his late 70's or early 80's. The mambunong appeared weak and fragile, but not too weak to carry out his task.

It was quite chill that night. I estimated the temperature to be about 15°C and so almost everyone was wearing some extra warm cloths, baseball caps, including the mambunong. The priest was wearing an old pants and a T-shirt and a torn black coat. His head was covered with an ordinary gray, unlabeled baseball cap. Other men and children were wearing baseball caps, some bearing labels 'NY' and 'Nike' logo in them while I was one of those few wearing a bonnet.

Coming back to the ceremony, as soon as the clothes of the deceased person were brought, the mambunong asked for rice wine (tapey) and an old lady brought some wine in an old iron mug. Once the mambunong received the wine, he muttered a relatively short prayer in native language squatting on the floor. The voice of the mambunong was so soft amid the noise from the surrounding crowd, chatting and laughing – as if they had nothing to do with the prayer - it was impossible to comprehend what the mambunong was saying. Even the research assistant Tamaken was able to comprehend no more than a few words and phrases. The researcher was able to catch a few words like 'anito, Kabunian' etc. The mambunong poured a little tapey on the ground, stood up, stretched his hands, and relaxed his legs. Meanwhile, a little further away, some young men were preparing a pig for slaughtering.

Once the priest finished the short prayer in the front-yard, he moved inside the house. The house had only one big hall and a portion of the hall was a kitchen. Once again squatting in the middle of the house, he continued to pray holding a black chicken in his hands. A cup of *tapey* was kept in front of him, which he poured on the ground once he finished the prayer. He handed over the chicken to be killed to a young man, who was sitting on the floor beside him.

The man who received the chicken started to kill the chicken by repeatedly hitting it with a small stick, assisted by his friends. The stick used, about half-a-meter long, was not something sanctified for that ritual or similar purpose but was an ordinary one. The same stick may have been used to beat disobedient children, or to drive away the unwanted cat or rat out of the house.

While the man was beating the chicken slowly and steadily to death, the research assistant commented that the style of killing is to keep the blood of the animal in the body to add flavour when cooked. It was later clarified by Ibaloy scholar Pungayan that the slow 'beating to death' is to show the significance of the offering, that is, the animal is offered alive, not as a dead animal.

Once the bird was beaten to death, the mambunong prayed once more, muttering scanty words. After his prayer, he got a cigarette from one of the men and smoked it inside the house. The cigarette seemed to be that of an ordinary commercial brand, Philip Morris. Of course, the smoking of cigarette is not part of the ritual, rather the priest wanted to relax a little bit in the cold night.

While staying inside the house, the attention of everyone was directed outside by the screaming sound of a pig. In the front yard a few young men started to slaughter a pig by slashing its neck with a big knife. Meanwhile, the native rice wine (tapey) was served to everyone, men, women and children. The researcher tasted the rice wine and found it similar to table wine, somewhat dry and flat in taste. The researcher also saw some men drinking 'San Miguel Gin' and was told by the research assistant that San Miguel Gin being a common drink among people sometimes replaces tapey in the rituals also.

The researcher was told that the bile of the butchered animal will be inspected by the mambunong, as it is customary, to certify that the animal is worthy of offering. If not, the mambunong would ask for another animal. When the butchered pig was cut into pieces, the mambunong was called to check the bile. Someone in the crowd pointed a flashlight and the mambunong checked seriously moving the spleen right and left to have a clear look. Once he saw it clearly, he accepted the animal as worthy for the sacrifice. The family who was hosting the cañao must have breathed a sigh of relief now, I thought. For, if the animal is not suitable, they have to look for another animal and it would be a Himalayan task in the midnight and a costly affair. Once the mambunong certified the butchered animal's worthiness, it was cooked without any other ingredients, a method called pinikpikan, in a big pot in the open space. In addition, rice was boiled in another pot.

By midnight, the researcher realized that there were around 60 to 70 people participating in the cañao. The people who gathered for the cañao were chatting, laughing, drinking and smoking in small groups.

Once the pinikpikan and rice was ready, an old woman put some rice on a plate, some boiled meat in a big aluminium bowl and a cup of tapey in the front-yard of the house. The mambunong joined by a few family members squatting on the ground uttered some prayers in his simple style. He poured some wine on the ground, as he had done earlier during prayers and the researcher understood that the prayer was over. It was then mealtime.

A few ladies served paper plates and two men (one carried rice, another meat) went around serving food wherever people were sitting or squatting. The mambunong joined a group of some old folks and tasted the meal. The researcher was told that it is the tradition to give one leg part of the butchered animal to the mambunong, and that is neither payment nor gift but his customary share. The researcher was served some food and tasted the pinikpikan. However, the researcher, being a vegetarian food lover, did not enjoy the pinikpikan due to its strong meat smell.

Once the meal was finished, swiftly a man started to check the pitch of a long native drum warming it near the fire in the place where food was prepared and two men started banging gongs. As soon as the musicians had discussed for a couple of minutes and had a minor rehearsal, they formed a circle and moved around playing the instruments. In addition to the drum and gongs, a fourth man played two metal pieces, complementing the beats of the drum and gongs. Some men and a few women joined the circle of musicians, dancing to the rhythm.

The researcher felt that the tapey and gin perhaps may have lowered the inhibition among the dancers; but learned later that this was not the case. The people have no inhibitions at all to dance; it is their culture and part of their life and in fact non-participation is often considered as apathetic.

The mambunong was given two blankets, thick and plain brown, appeared to be of native material, which he wore around his shoulders; he extended his hands and joined the dance. Women slightly bent their elbows as they danced without many articulations, while men extended their arms not bending their elbows much. A specific blanket worn by the one of the dancers was passed on to another person who is not dancing and that person join the dance.

The researcher was invited to dance but being too shy, declined to do so.

After about 20 to 30 minutes, the playing of music and the dancing stopped. Another set of dancing followed afterwards. The music was similar but not identical to the first one played. At this point the mambunong joined one of the smaller groups of men in conversation.

The series of music-and-dancing interspersed with short rest lasted until they all got sleepy at about 4:00 am.

Ifugao Wooden House

Chapter Eight

Cordillera People at the Crossroads

It is unfortunate that the early missionaries failed to appreciate the traditional worldview of the Cordillera people and forced them to abandon many of their age-old customs and traditions. .However the Cordilleran psyche and living still hovers around traditional culture, rituals and worldview

Change is an inevitable reality of life which permeates every sphere of human existence; in short, nothing remains the same. Humanity is a living witness to this constant flux in perception of reality around the globe as seen in progressive changes in belief systems, relationships, and existential issues. Today, it is virtually impossible for any culture or community to remain without change, completely isolated or without interaction with other cultures. The world is becoming smaller and smaller due to science and technology and there are hardly any community untouched by these forces of change and progress. As modern technological developments and the lifestyles of alien societies reach remote indigenous communities, centuries-old traditional customs fuse with the outside culture and new worldviews emerge. Interaction with an outside culture necessitates changes within one's own culture and civilization through adaptations and assimilations in accordance with the changing scenario.

When indigenous and non-indigenous groups meet, as McAdoo (1993) points out, acculturation and assimilation are the two processes that occur. Acculturation refers to the process whereby minority groups incorporate aspects of values and norms of the dominant culture into their own culture whereas assimilation is a blind adoption of whatever is seen in another culture (Mendoza, 1989).

What the indigenous people of the Cordilleras really need today is acculturation but in fact, what they are experiencing appears to be assimilation. Instead of becoming bicultural, that is, selectively adopting specific values while simultaneously retaining other time-proven traditional values and customs, they seem to succumb to the novelty of the Western and lowland Filipino culture through assimilation, partly due to Christian missionary and educational influence of the past. However, there is a strong awareness among many groups today about the need for acculturation. However, the reality is that because of assimilation, the vast traditional knowledge of the indigenous Cordillera people is endangered despite the many positive changes that the assimilation of alien cultures brought into the lives of the people.

The arrival of missionaries in the early 20th century and the rapidly increasing Christian denominations and religious sects with their generalized negative concepts that all traditional customary practices are superstitious and paganism have affected the Cordilleran people's traditional harmonious life with the nature. As a result, only elderly people administer traditional ritual healing and other customary ritual practices and even these are at the verge of disappearing into oblivion.

Inherently, in the Cordilleran psyche of both young and old, still appears to have a strong grip on their traditional doctrines, beliefs and conceptions in spite of many decades of foreign influence. This inherited traditional belief is the product of a continuous genetic informational flow in reproduction which is identified by Freud as "archaic inheritance" and Carl Jung as "collective unconscious". Jung (1968) explains collective unconscious as follows:

> "It is the mind of our unknown ancestors, their way of thinking and feeling, their way of experiencing life and the world, gods and men. The existence of these archaic strata is presumably the source of man's belief in reincarnations and in memories of 'previous existences' " (pp. 286-7).

This notion of inherent cultural concepts is further explained by Richard Dawkins, who coined the word "*meme*" in his book *The Selfish Gene* to identify this phenomenon. Dawkins defines '*meme*' as a unit of intellectual or cultural information, which is metaphorically equivalent to genes (Watson, 1995). Just as genes transmit biological genetic qualities from generation to generation, *memes* carry culture from generation to generation. They are passed on both vertically to the next generation and horizontally to others in community. However, today in the Cordilleran psyche, this fusion of inherited cultural values and the adoption, assimilation or intrusion of other cultures have created confusion rather than solace, dilemma rather than solution to their existential problems, ultimately resulting in questioning the validity of their own traditional wisdom.

Moving away from traditional, native philosophy of life and adopting a foreign culture prematurely can create many dilemmas in the life of the people. The younger generation move away from farm lands and settle for blue-collar and white-collar jobs which sometimes expose them to new economic hardships. From an ecological point of view, they become negligent in the care and nurture of nature and the natural resources around them; from a social point of view there is the devaluation of traditional values, interpersonal relationships and the inability to adapt to new-fangled life situations. They become completely dependent on another culture to the extent of losing their own identity and, from a psychological point of view there are many predicaments and amplified anxiety in facing existential issues.

Traditionally the elders in the indigenous Cordilleran communities passed on their knowledge of history, culture and belief system by living and working with their children. Today, migration to urban areas in pursuit of education and employment has reduced this possibility. Moreover, mass media like radio and television have penetrated the remotest areas of the mountains and traditional wisdom is slowly vanishing from the scene. The elderly people remain in the villages to tend to property and manage crops whereas the younger generation migrates to the metropolis and big cities and acculturate to the norms and values of their new environments, which gradually push traditional ways irrelevant in their lives.

Since indigenous Cordillera people consider themselves as an integral part of nature, there is an unconscious craving to live in total harmony with nature. Unlike the worldviews of the Western capitalists, the indigenous peoples' view of nature is that it is something not to be dominated but rather accepted, adopted and appreciated. The pressing threats to the harmonious life of the Cordillera people come mainly from two sources: a) the mushrooming Christian sects, and b) the culture-insensitivity of the Western educational system. Therefore, to preserve and nurture the traditional wisdom and harmonious life, these two institutions should work together. Most traditional communities are Christianized or being Christianized by different Christian denominations and the elders have less opportunity or no opportunity to transmit their cultural knowledge, which is often forbidden by the Christian sects. In addition, the so-called progressive lowland Filipino societies consider indigenous peoples and their native customs, beliefs and living as pagan, primitive and less progressive (Medina, 2000; Pungayan & Picpican, 1978). As a result, the younger generations look with contempt their own native culture and blindly adopt new lifestyles, beliefs and customs. An occupational therapy student from Baguio even declined to reveal her identity that she belongs to *Ibaloy* community. One sexagenarian lady from Mt. Province burst out, "Go and tell the people in the lowland, we are not eating grass; we are eating bread and rice; wearing clothes like them, we watch TV and live in comfortable houses as they do".

Western culture, religion and education which are introduced to indigenous Cordillera people by Christian missionary organizations of different denominations, has supplemented enormously the traditional cultural practices since the early 20th century. The humanitarian works of the missionaries are commendable; their early efforts in bringing education and medical facilities gave the Cordillera people comforts, convenience and economical security in their lives. On the other side, these missionary organizations introduced competing practices into indigenous societies with the primary objective of "civilizing" and Christianizing the "pagan" populations and remove their 'animistic' primitive practices (Medina, 2000).

It is a great pity that early Catholic missionaries forbade most of the indigenous Cordilleran practices. In the Mt. Province, a middle-aged lady explained that a missionary priest refused to enter her house to recite prayers because the feathers of chicken from a *cañao* were kept on the doorposts. The early missionaries even forbade the people to wear the traditional dress during liturgy and other Church functions, lamented an old lady from Ifugao. Ganggangan, Chancellor of the Benguet-Baguio Catholic Vicariate attributes this non-acceptance of traditional indigenous Cordilleran practices by the early missionaries in a mild way:

> "The 'eye glasses' they had [early missionaries] when they were sent as missionaries were very different; they saw realities with what they had been given at that time they were sent. After Vatican II and in recent times, we [Catholic Church] have better 'eye glasses' due to anthropological researches, acceptance of scientific methods and better scriptural interpretations and hermeneutics by Biblical scholars. However, it is not the case with many fanatical Christian denominations even today".

A vast majority of the Cordillera people have embraced Christianity. However, a greater part of the people follow a conflated version of religion that accepts Christ or any other Christian deity, and also accepts and acknowledges nature spirits and ancestral spirits and Christian spirits like angels, devils and saints. Many similarities can be drawn between the Cordillera concept of nature spirits both benevolent and malevolent ancestral spirits with the Christian belief in angels, devils and saints. Benevolent spirits can be compared to angels that guard and guide us. Malevolent spirits are like devils that cause us troubles, sickness and evils. Saints are similar to the deceased ancestral spirits, who guide and direct our daily life.

It is unfortunate that the early missionaries failed to appreciate this traditional worldview and forced the people to abandon many of their age-old customs and traditions such as, wearing the traditional dress, traditional music, *cañao* and other traditional festivals. Most of the Christian denominations make use of English and *Illocano* language (a low-land Filipino language) even today as the language of liturgy and as a result the native languages are at the verge of extinction. Instead of eradicating the traditional customs and practices in the name of God and evangelization, the missionaries can focus more on spreading the Christian values rather than Western culture and strengthen the traditional natural social cohesiveness. Indigenization is more than just understanding them so that one can effectively spread Christian values without eradicating the traditional wisdom of the people. This paradigm shift is necessary to preserve the Cordilleran identity. The focal point of this shift should therefore pave way for better understanding and acceptance of Cordillera indigenous worldview and help people to live fully in their own worldview.

In addition, the country's educational system which is fully Westernized should focus on integration instead of alienating the indigenous peoples from their own culture, identity and heritage. For example, in religion class, teach them the theology of *Kabunianism,* for nursing teach them to use the herbal medicines of Cordillera; in physical education integrate their traditional dance; in music give more emphasis on the use of the Cordilleran musical instruments and tunes etc.

All of the pressures the younger generations are exposed to confuses them and places them in a dilemma as to what to do in times of trouble. Thus, they are torn between the inherent traditional wisdom of their ancestors and the adopted western knowledge and culture. The beliefs, customs and traditions that gave solace to their elders for generations are downplayed by this fusion. Consequently, the emerging worldview places them between the threshold of two worlds often causing bewilderment especially in times of illness, pain, danger and related existential issues. Although the Catholic Church today encourages acculturation in many forms and means, the scope of the conflict is obvious.

.

Chapter Nine

Summary

In the name of God, missionaries introduced stereotypic concepts that being intuitive and one with the nature are indications of lack of education, superstition, primitive thinking, wishful fantasies, and emotional immaturity. Thus, they forbad traditional rituals and created confusion in the minds of the people and museumized Kabunianism.

Today the West is moving towards a greater appreciation of nature and the transcendental world. A good example of this in the field of psychology would be the various new branches of psychology like environmental psychology, transpersonal psychology etc... The efforts taken by classical psychologists like Carl Jung, Abraham Maslow, Stanislav Grof, Jane Roberts, Charles Tart, Ken Wilber and many others are slowly ripping and ready for harvest. Psychology that evolved purely into a scientific study in 1879 by Wilhelm Wundt and latter strengthened by behaviorists J. B. Watson, B. F. Skinner and others is losing its attraction today because of the emergence of transpersonal psychology and its various applications. In tune with this, transpersonal psychotherapy gives importance to spiritual, transpersonal and subjective interpretations of client's sufferings and concepts of healings in their therapeutic interactions and healing modalities. Western psychology, thus, is slowly incorporating a multidimensional view of psyche and the related realities which are accessible only through extraordinary states of consciousness. In addition to our five physical senses, the inner senses which are often talked by the mystics, sages, and seers of different Eastern traditions are gradually being recognized in Western psychology. This includes the use of direct subjective experience, deep intuitions and emotions together with intellect and reason.

The indigenous Cordillera people today tend to move from traditional tie-up towards Christianity and, from intuition to scientific outlook. This is the outcome of a range of stereotypic beliefs introduced and reinforced by the Christian missionaries in the name of religion that being intuitive and one with the nature are indications of lack of education, superstition, primitive magical thinking, wishful fantasies, and emotional immaturity. As modern cultures and technologies spread around the world, the extent of the knowledge store of native peoples is diminished continually. As older generations pass away, the younger generations happily adopt new life styles. They fail to understand that the native indigenous wisdom found in traditional resources, customs and practices are useful for interpersonal relationships, communitarian values, mental health and wellbeing. Native cultural values, knowledge and traditions which are subsumed by the domination of alien cultures that notoriously fosters different value system will create a vacuum in the thought and actions of people. Rather than just mourn over such a tide of assimilation, Cordillera people can be shown ways and means of digging out the treasures of their ancient wisdom so that they can benefit from its preservation as well as modification and practice. Many researchers are now placing a greater emphasis on recording indigenous cultures and knowledge; organizations are being formed to preserve and foster traditional cultures, language and knowledge of various groups of indigenous peoples.

The emerging worldview on healing practices studied as a cultural phenomenon opens new chapters in understanding the inner psyche, the psychic dilemmas, the conscience crisis the indigenous Cordillera people undergo constantly because of the influx of different cultures. On the other hand, examining the non-professional healing practices that are existing among the indigenous Cordillera people can open new vistas for integrating indigenous belief systems into mainstream culture-specific psychotherapy. This will give therapists a new perspective in understanding and helping patients coming from diverse cultural backgrounds, because the whole field of medicine is dominated by Western doctrines, theories and frameworks.

Today there is an increasing interest in the role of customs and cultural traditions in the healthcare disciplines because they influence human behaviors and health concepts. DSM-IV implies that all clinicians should be able to culturally explain cliental problems. It enjoins therapists to have more knowledge about the cliental culture and become flexible in their approaches. Therefore every therapist should be a multicultural specialist with a sound knowledge on cultural concepts, ethnic identities, and develop unique approaches and set of techniques that are consonant with the cultural belief system of their clients. Cultural psychology elevates the need for cultural relativism in psychotherapy by focusing on the cultural influences on the psychological process. In this context Bruner (1990) argues,

"Scientific psychology . . . will achieve a more effective stance toward the culture at large when it comes to recognize that the folk psychology of ordinary people is not just a set of self- assuaging illusions, but the culture's beliefs and working hypotheses about what makes it possible and fulfilling for people to live together. . . It is where psychology starts and wherein it is inseparable from anthropology" (p. 32).

Many traditional Cordilleran healing practices, especially for pneumasomatic sicknesses are based on supernatural, spiritual, or magical beliefs that go in tune with their worldview. These methods sometimes prove the power of belief, or work as a placebo effect. Treatments such as butchering of animals and praying, *cañao* etc., do work as cure, due to the power of belief in ritualism and the strong expectation of divine interventions during rituals. The more pneumasomatic the illness, the more probable is the cure. One important factor is that the healer and the healee have similar worldview and frame of mind, believe in the power of treatment that effect the cure.

In order to save the indigenous Cordillera culture and to integrate the salient features of their healing practices the following deliberations are made:

1. Cordillera religion can easily be classified as Kabunianism because of its systematic cosmic worldview.

2. Indigenous Cordillera people consider many of their illnesses to be caused by spirits; disorders that do not have organic basis are pneumasomatic sickness, spirits causing sickness in the body.

3. Even if the sickness is caused by bio-chemical factors and cured by western medicines and medical doctors,

customary rituals and prayers give inner solace that increase the recuperative power for quicker healing.

4. Healing is not a by-product of any specific technique used by the healer, or the healer is not as an authority or an active agent to "fix the client's problem" but rather as a chosen person to invoke divine interventions. Therefore some religious practices like prayer and customary rituals become active agents of therapy, resulting cure.

5. Western-type of psychotherapy training does not provide enough skills for therapists to encounter clients with different worldviews. In view of enhancing multicultural and culture-specific approach, immersion into different cultural setting for specific periods can be introduced in the regular curriculum or in internship programs for aspiring therapists.

6. The healer and healee holding the same worldview and mind-frame in understanding problems and illnesses may cause a placebo effect or body- mind connection that in turn increases recuperative power resulting cure.

7. The indigenous Cordillera people's unique cosmic worldview, health concepts and healing practices originating from their traditional wisdom were largely ignored or dismissed by Western education and Christian religions. The government and local bodies need to work hard to safeguard traditional identity of Cordillera people otherwise shortly their culture can become a museum piece.

8. Even though some of the findings of this study, when examined critically could be categorized as disappearing folklore, they are still considered by the indigenous Cordillera people as effective means of therapy. In view of this, counselors and psychotherapists who work for the benefit of the indigenous people and similar communities should utilize cultural therapy modalities as alternative or complementary therapies. What is superstition in one culture need not be a superstition in another culture!

References

Anderson, D. A. & Worthen, D. (1997).Exploring a fourth dimension: Spirituality as a resource for the couple therapist. *Journal of Marital and Family Therapy, 23*(1), 3-12.

Angelo, J. & Reyes, A. (1987). *Igorot: A people who daily touch the earth and the sky Ethnographies of major tribes.* Baguio: Cordillera Schools Group.

Bailey, A. (1925). *A treatise on cosmic fire.* New York, NY: Lucis Publishing Company

Becker, P. H. (1993). Common pitfalls in published grounded theory research. *Qualitative Health Research, 3,* 254-260.

Bengwayan, G. (19?). *A case study of indigenous florae diversity conservation practices inLusod, Kabayan, Benguet.* Paper presented at the meeting held in La Trinidad, Benguet State University.

Benor, D. J. (1993).*Healing Research.* Munich/ Oxford: Helix.

Benor, D. J. (1994).Hands-on help, *Nursing Times, 90*(44), 28-29.

Benor, D. J. (1994 a).Spiritual healing and psychotherapy. *The Therapist, 4*(1), 37-39.

Benor, D. J. (1999).*Holistic Integrative Care.* Retrieved October 20, 2001 from http://www.wholistichealingresearch.com/Articles/WholisIC.htm

Benor, D.J. (2001). Spiritual Healing for Mental Health. In: Shannon, S. (Ed.),*Handbook of complementary and alternative therapies in mental health,* San Diego, CA: Academic/Harcourt (pp 258-267).

Benson, H. (1996). *Timeless healing: The power and biology of belief.* NY: Scribner Press.

Bergin, A.E., & Payne, R. (1991).Proposed agenda for a spiritual strategy in personality and psychotherapy. *Journal of Psychology and Christianity, 10*(3), 197-210.

Blunt, W., & Raphael, S. (1979). *The illustrated herbal.* New York: Thames & Hudson, Inc.

Bontengan, K. C. (1994). *Bontoc concepts on illness and death.* Quezon City: Giraffe Books.

Boyle J. S., & Andrews M. M. (1995).*Trans-cultural concepts in nursing care* (2nded.). J.B. Philadelphia: Lippincott Company.

Bruner, J. (1990). *Acts of meaning.* Cambridge: Harvard University Press.

Bugental S. J., & Pierson, F. (Eds.). (2001).*Handbook of humanistic psychology.* CA: Sage Publications, Ltd.

Bulatao, J. (1992). *Phenomena and their interpretation.* Manila: Ateneo de Manila University Press.

Calpotura, V. S. (2000). Counseling and the Christian spiritual tradition of spiritual direction. "In" Clemeña (Ed.), *Counseling in Asia* (pp. 85 - 90). Manila: De La sale University Press.

Campbell, J. (1984).*The way of the animal powers.* New York: Harper and Row.

Castillo, R .J. (1997).Cultural assessment."In" R. J. Castillo, *Culture and mental illness* (pp. 55-75). Pacific Grove, CA: Brooks/Cole.

Chein, I. (1981). Appendix: An introduction to sampling. "In" L. H. Kidder, *Research methods in social relations.* (4thed.). (pp. 418-441). New York: holt, Rinehart, & Winston.

Chrisman, L. (2001). Native American medicine: *Gale Encyclopaedia of*

Alternative Medicine. Gale Group.

Claver, F. (1995).*The social marginalization of tribal peoples and their contribution to ecological health.* A report delivered in a conference on the concerns of indigenous peoples, HuaHin, Thailand.

Clemeña, R. M. (1993). *Counseling psychology in the Philippines: Research and practice*. Manila: De La Salle University Press.

Cohen, C. P (1996).*Human rights of indigenous peoples*. NY: Transnational Pub.

Cole, M. (1996).*Cultural psychology: A once and future discipline.* Cambridge, MA: Harvard University Press.

Cooperstein, M. A. (1992). The myths of healing: A summary of research into transpersonal healing experience. *Journal of the American Society for Psychical Research,86,* 99-133.

Cusani, M. (2002).Health and illness in types. *Enneagram Monthly, 8*(6) Retrieved on January 14, 2003 from http://www.ideodynamic.com/enneagrammonthly/EM_archiv.htm?2002/ EM_0206_a1.htm

Daniels, M. (1997).Holism, integration and the transpersonal. *Transpersonal Psychology Review, 1(3), 12-16.*

*Daniels, M. (1998).*Transpersonal psychology and the paranormal. *Transpersonal Psychology Review, 2(3),* 17-31.

Davis, J. (2001). *What is transpersonal psychology*. Retrieved October 13, 2001 from http://clem.mscd.edu/~davisj/tp/what1.html

Demetrio, F., Gilda C.F., & Zialcita, F. (1991).*The soul book.* Quezon City: GCF Books.

Duckro, P. N., Busch, C., McLaughlin, L. J., & Schroeder, J. (1992).

Psychotherapy with religious professionals: An aspect of the interface of psychology and religion. *Psychological Reports, 70*, 304-306.

Edman, J. L., & Kameoka, V. A. (1997). Cultural differences in illness schemas: An analysis of Filipino and American ill attributions. *Journal of Cross-Cultural Psychology*, *28*(3), 252-266.

Enriquez, V. (1977).Filipino psychology in the Third World. *Philippine Journal of Psychology, 10*, 3- 18.

Enriquez, V. (1993).Towards a Filipino counseling philosophy. In Clemeña (Ed.), *Counseling psychology in the Philippines: Research and practice* (pp. 9-18) Manila: De La Salle University Press.

Fehring, R. J., Brennan, P. F., & Keller, M. L. (1987).Psychological and spiritual well-being in college students. *Research in Nursing and Health, 10,* 391-398.

Fox, R. B. (1978). *Tagbanwa heaven in Filipino heritage*. Manila: Lahing Pilipino Publisher.

Frankl, V. E. (1967). *Psychotherapy and existentialism*. NY: Washington Square Press.

Frazer. J. G. (1968). *The belief in immortality and the worship of the dead* (3 vol.). London: Unsworth's Booksellers.

Freedman, S. R., Enright, R. D. (1996).Forgiveness as an intervention goal with incest survivors. *Journal of Counseling and Clinical Psychology, 64*, 983-992.

Freud, S. (1928). *The future of an illusion*. London: Hogarth Press.

Fullilove, R. E., &Fullilove, M. T. (1995). Community disintegration and public health: A case study of New York City. *Assessing the social and behavioral science base for HIV/AIDS prevention and intervention:*

Workshop summary. Washington, DC: Institute of Medicine.

Funk, K. (2001). *What is a worldview?* Retrieved August 28, 2002 from http://www.engr.orst.edu/~funkk

Gett, T. K. (1995). *Collecting ethnographic data: The ethnographic interview*. Retrieved Jan 12, 2003 from http://ethnomed.org

Ghosh, A. (1994). *Oraon worldviews and concepts of health and medicine*. In *Man in India, 76*(1): 67-80.

Glaser, B. G. (1978). *Theoretical sensitivity: Advances in the methodology of grounded theory*. Mill Valley, CA: Sociology Press.

Glaser, B. G., & Strauss, A. L. (1967).*The discovery of grounded theory*. Chicago: Aldine.

Glaser, B. G. (1992). *Basis of grounded theory analysis: Emergence versus forcing*. California: Sociology Press.

Goldberg, J. R. (1994, June). Spirituality, religion and secular values: What role in psychotherapy? *AAMFT Family Therapy News*, pp. 9, 16-17.

Gordon, M. M. (1978). *Human nature, class, and ethnicity*. New York, NY: Oxford   University Press.

Griffiths, B. (1982). *Marriage of East and West.* London: Templegate.

Gudykunst, W. B. (1997). Cultural variability in communication. *Communication Research, 24* (4): 327-348.

Halifax, J. (1982). *Shaman-The wounded healer*. New York: Crossroads Publishing.

Halstead, M. T., & Fernsler, J. I. (1994).Coping strategies of long-term cancer survivors. *Cancer Nursing, 17*(2), 94-100.

Headland, T. N. Pike K. L., & Harris M. (1990). (Ed.). *"Emics" and*

"Etics": The insider/outsider debate. London: Sage Publications.

Helfrich, P. (2002) *The emerging new worldview: An introduction and overview*. Retrieved November 13, 2002 from http://www.newworldview.com

Hendricks, G., & Weinhold, B. (1982).*Transpersonal approaches to counseling and psychotherapy*. London: Love Publishing Company.

Hewson, M. G. (1998). Traditional healers in Southern Africa.*Annals of Internal Medicine, 128*, 1029-1034.

Heyink, J. W., & Tymstra, T. (1993).The function of qualitative research. *Social Indicators Research, 29*, 291-305.

Hodes, R. M. (1997). Cross-cultural medicine and diverse health beliefs: Ethiopians abroad. *Western Journal of Medicine, 166*, 29-36.

Hodge, J. L., Struckmann, D. K.; and Trost, L. D. (1975).*Cultural bases of racism and group oppression*. CA: Two Riders Press.

Hultkrantz, A. (1992). *Shamanic healing and ritual drama.* NY: Crossroad.

Ibrahim, F. A. (1985). Effective cross-cultural counseling and psychotherapy: A framework. *The Counseling Psychologist, 13,* 625 – 638.

James, W. (1936).*The varieties of religious experience*. NY: Modern Library.

Janetius, S. T. (2010). *Delusive healing: Implications for Indigenous Therapeutic Counselling in India,* Retrieved November12, 2014 from http://janetius.page.tl/Delusive-healing.htm

Jung, C. G. (1958). *The collected works of C. G. Jung* (vol. II). Princeton, NJ: Princeton University Press.

Jung, C. G. (1968). *The archetypes and the collective unconscious.* Princeton: Princeton University Press.

Jung, C. G. (1989). *Memories, dreams, reflections.* Vancouver: Vintage Books.

Kasprow, M. C., & Scotton B. W. (1999).A review of transpersonal theory and its application to the practice of psychotherapy. *Journal of Psychotherapy Research and Practice,. 8,* 12-23.

Kemf, E. (1993). *The law of the mother: Protecting indigenous peoples and protected areas.* San Francisco: Sierra Books.

Kleinman, A. (1988). *The illness narratives: Suffering, healing and the human condition.* New York: Basic Books.

Klimesh M. (2001). *Shamanism - Medicine men and priests.* Retrieved October 4, 2001 from http://www.ubook.org/esg/esg090.html

Krippner, S. (1988). Shamans: The first healers. In G. Doore (Ed.), *Shaman's path: Healing, personal growth and empowerment* (pp. 101-114). Boston, MA: Shambala Publications.

Knudtson, P., & Suzuki, D. (1992).*Wisdom of the elders.* Toronto: Stoddart Publishing Ltd.

Lacanaria, M. C. (1999). *Health beliefs and practices of the Ibalois of Kabayan.* Unpublished master's thesis, Baguio City, Saint Louis University.

Lacanaria, M. C. (2000). Ibaloi beliefs and behaviors on health and illness.*SLU Research Journal,31,* (2), 281-318.

Lajoie, D. H., & Shapiro, S. I. (1992). Definitions of transpersonal psychology: The first twenty-three years. *Journal of Transpersonal Psychology, 24*(1), 79-98.

Lambrecht, F. (1978).Adaptation of Ifugao local customs in Christianity.*SLU Research Journal, 9,* (3-4), 327 – 351.

Layder, D. (1982). Grounded theory: A constructive critique. *Journal for the Theory of Social Behavior 12*, 103-123.

Leininger, M. M. (1985). *Qualitative research methods in nursing.* New York: Grune& Stratton, Inc.

Leininger, M. M. (1991). *Culture care diversity and universality: A theory of nursing.* New York: National League for Nursing Press.

Leininger, M. M. (1997). Overview and reflection of the theory of culture care and the ethno-nursing method. *Journal of Trans-cultural Nursing, 8* (2), 32–52.

Leith, M. (2003).*The three worldviews framework.* Retrieved January 13, 2003 from http://www.martinleith.com/worldviews/welcome.html

LeShan, L. (1995). *The medium, the mystic, and the physicist : Toward a general theory of the paranormal.* New York: Penguin.

Levey, M. (1966).*The medical formulary or aqrabadhin of Al-Kindi.* Madison: The University of Wisconsin Press.

Levin. J. S. (1998). From psychosomatic to theosomatic: The role of spirit in the next new paradigm. *Subtle Energies and Energy Medicine* 9(1),1-26.

Levin, J. S., Larson, David B., & Puchalski, M., (1997). Religion and spirituality in medicine: Research and education. *Journal of the American Medical Association 278*, 792-793.

Lincoln, Y. S., & Guba E. G. (1985).*Naturalistic inquiry.* Newbury Park, CA: Sage Publication.

Manoleas, P. (1996). Culture and case management. "In" Manoleas (Ed.),

The cross-cultural practice of clinical case management in mental health (pp. 1-40). Binghamton, NY: Haworth Press, Inc.

Mata, E. Q. (1952). *An analysis of the folk dances of the mountain province and the possibility of their inclusion in the physical education program.* Unpublished master's thesis, Baguio, Baguio colleges.

McAdoo, H. P. (1993). Ethnic families: Strengths that are found in diversity. "In" McAdoo (Ed.), *Family ethnicity: Strength in diversity* (pp. 3-14). CA: Sage Publications.

Medina, C. R. (2000). *C.I.C.M. missionaries and indigenous Filipinos.* Baguio City: St. Louis University Press.

Mendoza, R. H. (1989). An empirical scale to measure type and degree of acculturation in Mexican-American adolescents and adults. *Journal of Cross-Cultural Psychology, 20*(4), 372-385.

Michael, D. (2001). *What is transpersonal psychology?* Retrieved October 14, 2001 from http://www.mdani.demon.co.uk/trans/tranintro.htm

Miller, J. (1982). Asian religions. *Focus on Asian Studies, 2,* (1), 26-27.

Miller, J. S. (1990). Mental illness and spiritual crisis: Implications for psychiatric rehabilitation. *Psychosocial Rehabilitation Journal, 14*(2), 29-47.

Murdock, G. P. (1980). *Theories of illness: A world survey.* Pittsburgh: University of Pittsburgh Press.

Natocyad, E. (1998). *Indigenous healing: A journey back to our indigenous roots.* Unpublished master's thesis, Manila, Asian Social Institute.

Offiong, D. (1999). Traditional healers in the Nigerian health care delivery system and the debate over integrating traditional and scientific medicine. *Anthropological Quarterly*, *72*(3), 118-131.

Orallo, M. C. (1999). *Benguet Kankana-ey wedding, death, illness prayer rituals: Socio-cultural concepts and poetic devices.* Unpublished master's thesis, Baguio City, Saint Louis University.

Orr, D. W. (1994). *Earth in mind: On education, environment and the human prospect.* Washington, D.C.: Island Press.

Oxman, T. E., Freeman, D. H., & Manheimer, E. D. (1995).Lack of social participation or religious strength and comfort as risk factors for death after cardiac surgery in the elderly. *Psychosomatic Medicine, 57*(1), 5 - 15.

Pachter, L. M., Cloutier, M. M., & Bernstein, B. A. (1995).Ethno-medical (folk) remedies for childhood asthma in a mainland Puerto Rican community. *Archives of Paediatrics and Adolescent Medicine*, *149*(9), 982-989.

Padang, B. D. (1983*). A case study of the political culture among the Bontoc Tribe.* Unpublished master's thesis, Baguio City, Saint Louis University.

Panos, P. T., & Panos, A. J. (2000).A model for a culture-sensitive assessment of patients in health care settings. *Social Work in Health Care, 31*(*1), 49-62.

Pelto, P. J., & Pelto. G. H. (1978). Units of observation: "Emic" and "Etic" approaches. "In" *Anthropological research: The structure of inquiry.* Cambridge: Cambridge University Press.

Picpican, I., & Guinaran, E. C. (1981).Folk medicine among Benguet Igorots. *St. Louis University Research Journal, 12* (1), 93-123.

Potts, R. G. (1996). Spirituality and the experience of cancer in an

African-American community: Implications for psychosocial oncology. *Journal of Psychosocial Oncology, 14*(1), 1-19.

Prest. L. A., & Keller, J. F. (1993). Spirituality and family therapy: Spiritual beliefs, myths, and metaphors. *Journal of Marital and Family Therapy, 19*(2), 137-148.

Pungayan, E., & Picpican, I. (1978). Rituals and worship among the BenguetIgorots. *St. Louis University Research Journal, 9* (3-4), 460-493.

Ramakrishna, J., & Weisss, M.G. (1992). Health, illness, and immigration: East Indians in the United States. *The Western Journal of Medicine, 157*(3), 265-271.

Ramos, E. (1995). *Cordillera women weaving the life blanket.* 4th world conference on women, Asian women's human rights council, Beijing. Retrieved October 16, 2001 from http://ourworld.compuserve.com/homepages/edessaramos/Cordillera.html

Raposas, T. (1999). In Baguio, healing is believing. Retrieved January 7, 2003 from http://www.atimes.com/se-asia/AI22Ae02.html

Richards, P. S., & Bergin, A. E. (1997).*A Spiritual strategy for counseling and psychotherapy*. Washington, D.C.: American Psychological Association.

Riordan, C. M., & Vandenberg, R. J. (1994). A central question in cross-cultural research: Do employees of different cultures interpret work-related measures in an equivalent manner? *Journal of Management, 20,* 643-671.

Ruiz, N. (2000). Moving towards a culture specific counseling model for Asia. "In" Clemeña (Ed.), *Counseling in Asia,* (pp. 1-5). Manila: De La Salle University Press.

Salazar, Z. (1996). The Babaylan in Philippine History. In *Women's role in Philippine history: Selected essays* (2nd ed.). Manila: The University of the Philippine Press.

Santos, D. (1998). Multicultural perspective in three international schools in the Philippines. "In" Bernado, (Ed.), *Understanding behavior bridging cultures* (pp 159-166). Manila: De La Salle University Press.

Scott, W. H. (1975). *History of the Cordillera*. Baguio City: Baguio Printing & Publishing Co., Inc.

Scott, R. W., & Meyer, J. W. (1994).*Institutional environments and organization: Structural complexity and individualism*. London: Sage Publication.

Sevilla, J. C. (1995). Indigenous research methods: Evaluating first returns. "In" Pe. (Ed.) *Filipino Psychology: Theory, method and application* (pp. 221 – 232). Manila: University of the Philippines Press.

Shweder, R., & Bourne, E. (1982). Do conceptions of the person vary cross-culturally? In A. Marsella & G. White (Eds.), *Cultural conceptions of mental health and therapy* (pp. 97-137). Dordrecht: Reidel.

Sianghio, C. (2002). *Ifugao.* Retrieved February 23, 2002 from http://litera1no4.tripod.com/ifugao_frame.html

Sigerist, H. E. (1951). *A history of medicine.* New York: Oxford University Press.

Silva, R. (2001).*What is transpersonal psychology?* Retrieved October 14, 2001 from http://www.cyberpsychologist.com

Sollod, N. R. (1993). *Comprehensive handbook of psychotherapy and integration.* New York: Plenum Press.

Stone, E. (2002). *Ancient techniques, modern journeys: Shamanic journeys and psychotherapy.* Retrieved January 18, 2002 from http://www.boulder.net/~estone/ancient_techniques.html

Strauss, A., & Corbin, J. (1990).*Basics of qualitative research: Grounded theory, procedures and techniques.* Newbury Park, CA: Sage Publications.

Stuart (2002).*Alternative medicine in the Philippines*. Retrieved February 04, 2002 from http://stuartxchange.com/AltMedIntro.html

Sullivan, W.P. (1993). It helps me to be a whole person: The role of spirituality among the mentally challenged. *The Psychosocial Rehabilitation Journal, 16*(3), 125-134.

Tart, C. (1987).*Waking up: Overcoming the obstacles to human potential.* Boston: Shambala.

Tishelman, C., & Sachs, L. (1998).The diagnostic process and the boundaries of normality. *Qualitative Health Research, 8*(1), 48–61.

Trimble, J. E. (2000). Considering the cultures within. Retrieved October 14, 2001 from http://www.radcliffe.edu/quarterly/200004/hidden-6.html

Turner, R. P., Lukoff, D., Barnhouse, R. T., & Lu, F. G. (1995).Religious or spiritual problem. A culturally sensitive diagnostic category in the DSM-IV. *Journal of Nervous & Mental Disease. 183*(7), 435-444.

Valdez, M. H. (1993). *Reflections of culture in the folk songs of the BenguetIbalois.* Unpublished master's thesis, Baguio City, Saint Louis University.

Velasco, F. (2002).*Kankana-ey.* Retrieved February 25, 2002 from

http://litera1no4.tripod.com/kankanæy_frame.html

Veneracion, J. (1991). From Babaylan to Beata: A study on the religiosity of Filipino Women. *Review of Women's Studies, 3*, 1.

Villar, I. V. (1997). *Western approaches to counseling in the Philippines*. Manila: De La Salle University Press.

Walsh, B., & Middleton, R. (1984).*The transforming vision: Shaping a Christian worldview*. Downers Grove: IVP.

Walsh, R., & Vaughan, F. (Eds.). (1993). *Paths beyond ego: The transpersonal vision*. LA: Tarcher-Putnam.

Ward, K. (1987). *Images of eternity*. Oxford: One world.

Watson. L. (1995).*Dark nature. A natural history of evil*. London: Hodder& Stoughton.

Weil, A. (1995). *Spontaneous healing*. New York: Knopf.

White, N., & Lubkin, I. (1998). Illness trajectory. In I. M. Lubkin (Ed.), *Chronic illness: Impact and interventions* (4[th]ed.) (pp. 53-76). Sudbury, MA: Jones and Bartlett Publishers.

Wilber, K. (1977). *The spectrum of consciousness*. Wheaton: Quest.

Wilber, K. (1983). *A sociable god: Toward a new understanding of religion*. London: Shambhala.

Wilber, K. (2000). *Sex, ecology, spirituality: The spirit of evolution (*2nd rev. ed.). Boston: Shambhala.

Wurges, J. (2001). Shamanism. *Gale Encyclopaedia of Alternative Medicine*. Gale Group.

Yeo, A. (2000). Counseling trends in postmodernist thinking in counseling. "In" Clemeña (Ed.), *Counseling in Asia* (pp. 6-19). Manila: De La Salle University Press.

Znamenski, A. (2003). *Shamanism in Siberia: Russian records of indigenous spirituality* , Springer Publishers

About the Author

Janetius completed his Doctorate from De La Salle University, Manila, Philippines in Counseling Psychology, under the guidance of Dr Alexa Abrenica, studying the healing practices of Cordillera people in the Philippines. Living more than three years among the indigenous people in the Cordillera provinces, he experienced the daily lifestyle and existential issues of the people before completing his doctoral research. Presently he is the Head of the Department of Psychology and Director of Guidance and Counseling Services in an autonomous college in India.

He is a multidisciplinary researcher who has written and edited books on Culture and Higher Education in Ethiopia, Indian Higher Education Today, Human Rights Abuse on Elders, Rural Empowerment for Sustainable Development, and Visions in Mahabharata and Bible.

www.ingramcontent.com/pod-product-compliance
Lightning Source LLC
Chambersburg PA
CBHW050455290526
45786CB00006B/2308